When all the accounts are closed you need not be reborn. This is the philosophy of going beyond life and death. Then you need not be reborn again; you simply disappear from this phenomenal world, from this bodily, physical world. Then you exist as cosmos, not as individuals.

OSHO

VEDANTA:
The Supreme Knowledge

FUSION BOOKS

Co-ordination: Swami Amano Surdham
Compilation: Swami Yogesh
Editing: Ma Yoga Pratima
Design: Swami Prem Asang

ISBN : 81-8419-206-1

Published by
FUSION BOOKS
X-30, Okhla Industrial Area,
Phase - II, New Delhi - 110 020
Phone : 011-41611861
Fax : 011-41611866
E-mail : sales@diamondpublication.com
Website : www. dpb.in

Edition : **2010**

Printed by
Adarsh Printers, Navin Shahdara, Delhi-110032

Contents

OSHO

is another name for celebration, another expression for
benediction. He offers hope and confidence, love and
compassion, being and awareness to the human race
beleaguered by death and destruction, pain and suffering.
He is an invitation to experiencing a new rhythm in life,
a new dance, a new thrill in one's life.
To miss him is to miss
the greatest blessing.

OSHO

Never born
Never died
Only visited this planet earth from
December 11, 1931 to January 19, 1990

These discourses are his spontaneous responses to live
audience, are of eternal significance, and
concern one and all.

1

SUBLIME IS THE
SPONTANEOUS

There are two kinds of non-attachment: the ordinary and the sublime: That attitude of non-attachment to the objects of desire in which the seeker knows that he is neither the doer nor the enjoyer, neither the restrained nor the restrainer, is called ordinary non-attachment. He knows that whatever faces him in this life is the result of the deed of his past life. Whether in pleasure or in pain, he can do nothing. Indulgence is but a disease and affluence of all kinds a storehouse of adversity. Every union leads inevitably to separation. The ignorant suffer the maladies of mental anxiety. All material things are perishable, because time is constantly devouring them. Through the understanding of scriptural devouring them. Through the understanding of scriptural percepts, one's faith in material things is uprooted and one's mind freed of them. This is called ordinary non-attachment.

When thoughts like: ' I am not the doer, my past deeds are the doers, or God himself is the doer," cease to worry the seeker, a state of silence, equilibrium and peace is attained. This is called sublime non-attachment.

On the path, in the search, every step has two sides: the beginning of the step, and the conclusion. The beginning will always be with conscious effort; it is bound to be so. A struggle will be there, constant need to be alert will be there. Sometimes you will fall asleep, sometimes you will forget, sometimes you will go astray. Again and again you will have to remember, come back to the path. Again and again you will have to make more intense effort to be conscious.

So the beginning of every step will be struggle. There will be ups and there will be downs. Sometimes you will feel very miserable, frustrated. Whenever the contact with the method is lost, whenever you have gone astray, frustration will happen; you will feel depressed, sad, lost. There will be moments of intense happiness also. Whenever you regain the control again, whenever even for moments you become the master, whenever even for small glimpses you become capable, you will feel intense joy spreading all over your being.

Peaks and valleys will be there. They will disappear only when the conscious effort has disappeared, when the method is no more a method, when the method has become your very consciousness, when you need not remember it, When you can completely forget it and it still grows, continuous, flows, when you need not maintain it, when you need not even think of it- and then it becomes spontaneous, sahaj. This is the end aspect of every step. Remember this: through constant practice, a moment comes when you can drop the practice completely, and unless you can drop the practice, you have not attained.

Taoist masters have used many dimensions: poetry, painting, and many other crafts have been used as training grounds. Painting has been used for centuries in China and Japan. And Taoist painting has a principle, and that principle is that first one should become proficient in painting, in the technique of painting-it takes many years-and then for a few years one has to drop painting completely. One has to forget that one is a painter; throw the brushes, colours, inks, and just drop from the mind that one has learned something. For a few years one has to be completely away from painting. When the thought has dropped, then again the master says,' Now you start ! Now this man is not a technician. He knows the technique, but he is not a technician because there is no need to be aware of techniqe. Now he can paint like a small child. The effort has ceased; to paint has become effortless. Only then master-teachers are born.

I remember one story I would like to tell you. It happened once in Burma that a great temple was to be built, and the main door had to be something unique on the earth. So, many painters, Zen masters, Taoist masters, were asked, and one who was the greatest was invited to design the door. That great master had a habit that whenever he would paint something, design something, his chief disciple would sit by his side, and whenever he would complete the design, he would ask the chief disciple whether it was okay. If the disciple said no, he would throw the design and he would again work on it. Unless the disciple said," Right, this is the thing,' he would go on.

Designing this main gate of the temple became a problem, because the chief disciple continued to say no. The master painted at least one hundred designs; many months passed. He would work for weeks, and when the design was complete he would look at the disciple who was sitting beside him. The disciple would shake his head and he would say,'No,' and the master would put aside the design and start again. He was also worried, 'What is going to happen? When will this design be complete?' And he had been doing such hard work as he had never done in his life.

Then one day it happened. The ink with which he was painting was almost finished, so he told the disciple to go out of the house and prepare

Vedanta: The Supreme Knowledge

ink. The disciple went out to prepare the ink, and when he came back he started dancing in ecstasy and he said, 'Now this is the thing! But why couldn't you paint it before.'

The master said, 'Now I know. I was also worried. What was happening? Now I know—your presence was the disturbance. In your presence I remained the technician. I was aware that I was doing something, effort was there. I was conscious of the effort, and I was thinking, expecting, that this time you would says yes. That was the disturbance. I could not be spontaneous. When you went out I could forget you, and when I could forget you, I could forget myself also.'

Because the self is the reaction to the other. If the other is in yours consciousness, you will remain the ego. They both drop simultaneously: when the other has disappeared, the ego has disappeared.

'And when I was not,' the master said,' the painting flowed by itself. This design I have not done. All those hundred designs you rejected were my doings. This design is through Tao, through nature; it has dropped from the cosmos itself. I was just a vehicle. I could forget and become a vehicle.'

When you can forget the method, the effort, the self, the other; when everything has been dropped and you have become simply a flow of energy, spontaneous, then really something is attained, not before. And look at the difference in the Eastern and Western attitudes about

12

painting and about everything else also. In the west you have to make conscious effort, and bring the effort to peak. you become a technician and the other part is missing. In the East you have to become a technician, and then drop that whole technicality and become again innocent, simple, as if you were never trained.

Once somebody asked Winston Churchill one of the greatest orators the West has produced —'Don't you get afraid of the audience? Thousands of people staring at you——don't you get afraid, sacred? Don't you get a little fear inside?

Churchill said, 'This has been my constant practice: that whenever I stand to speak, I look at the audience and I think, "So many fools." The moment this thought comes to my mind I am okay, then I don't worry.'

Somebody asked the same question of Zen master, Rinzai,' You speak to thousand; don't you ever get worried about it? Don't you ever get scared? Don't you ever get an inner trembling? Because so many persons are present—judging, observing, looking at you.'

Rinzai said, 'Whenever I look at people, I say, "I am Sitting there also. Only I am in this hall." Then there is no problem. I am alone; these people are also me.'

This is the Eastern and Western difference. Churchill represents the West. If others are fools then you are okay, then the ego is strengthened.

You don't worry about them, because who are they?—nobodies. And Rinzai says, 'The other is not. They are just me, my forms. I am alone. I am the speaker, and I am also the audience. Then what is the fear?'

In your bathroom when you are alone, you can be a good singer—everybody is, almost everybody. And bring the same man out of the bathroom, let him stand here, and the moment he sees you he is no more capable of singing—even humming becomes impossible. The fear grips the throat: he is not alone, the others are there, they will judge. The moment the other is there, fear has entered. But the same man was humming beautifully, singing beautifully in the bathroom—nobody was there.

The same happens when you can see in the other your own self. Then the whole earth is your bathroom; you can sing, you can dance. The other is no more there, there is nobody to judge. Through these eyes you are looking, and through other's eyes also you are looking. Then it becomes a cosmic play of one energy in many forms. But the ultimate of any method is to become methodless; the ultimate of every technique is to become non-technical, innocent. All effort is only to attain an effortless spontaneity.

There are two kinds of non-attachment: the ordinary and the sublime.

The ordinary is the first aspect of *vairagya*, non-attachment. The sublime is the spontaneous, the end; the other aspect of the same when things have become spontaneous.

That attitude of non-attachment to the objects of desire in which the seeker knows that he is neither the doer nor the enjoyer, neither the restrained nor the restrainer, is called ordinary non-attachment.

The emphasis is on the words 'knows'. He has to maintain that, he has to remember it 'I am not the doer. I am just a witness. Whatsoever happens I am not involved. I am an outsider, just a spectator.' But this has to be remembered, this has to be maintained. This point must not be lost. And it is very difficult to remember it constantly. To remember even for a few minutes is difficult, because for many many lives you have been the doer, constantly you have been the enjoyer.

When you are eating, you are the eater; when you are walking, you are the walker; when you are listening, you are the listener. You have never made any effort to remember that while doing anything, you are not the doer, but the witness. While eating, try it. The food is going into the body, not into you. It cannot go into you, there is no way, because you are the consciousness, and the food cannot enter consciousness. It will go into the body, it will become the blood and the bone, whatsoever the body needs, but you remain a witness.

So while sitting at your table eating your food, don't be the eater. You have never been the eater; this is just an old habit, an old conditioning.

Look at the eater, the body, and the eaten, the food, and you be the third. You just witness, you just hover over, you just look from a distance. Stand aloof and see your body eating, the food being eaten, and don't get involved in it. But you can maintain it only for a few seconds—again you will become the eater. It has been such a long, long conditioning; it will take time to break it.

You are walking on the street. Don't be the walker, just watch the body walking. For a few seconds you may remember; again you will forget, and you will enter in the body and become the walker. But even if for a few seconds you can maintain it, you can remember that you are not the walker, then those few seconds will become satori-like, those few seconds will be weightless, those few seconds will be of such a joy you have never known. And if this can happen for a few seconds, why not for ever?

Somebody is insulting you. It will be more difficult than with walking or eating to remember that you are the witness. One Indian mystic, Ram Teerth, went to America in the beginning of this century. He never used the word 'I'; he would always use the name 'ram'. If he was hungry, he would say, 'Ram is hungry.' It looked unfamiliar and strange. If there was a headache, he would say, 'Ram has a headache.'

One day it happened that a few people insulted him. He came back laughing and his disciples asked, 'Why are you laughing?' So he said,'Ram was insulted very much, and I enjoyed. I was standing out of Ram and looking. Ram was in much difficulty; much inconvenience, discomfort, was there in Ram.'

You become an object of your own consciousness. This is coming out of the body, out of the ego, out of the mind. This is difficult not because it is unnatural; this is difficult only because of long conditioning. You may have observed that small babies, in the beginning never say 'I'. They say, "Baby is hungry.' They seem to be witnessing the phenomenon. But we train them to use the 'I', because it's not good to say,'Baby is hungry,' or 'baby wants to play.' We train them to use the 'I'.

'I' is not existential. 'I' is a social entity; it has to be created, it is just like language. It is needed, because if people go on speaking like babies, or like Ram Teerth; if , like Ram Teerth, people go on saying their names, it will be very difficult to say whatever they are talking about themselves or about somebody else. It will create confusion. If you say, 'I am hungry,' immediately it is meant that you are hungry. If you say, 'Ram is hungry,'If people know that you are Ram then it's okay, otherwise they will think somebody else is hungry, not you. And if everybody uses it, it will create confusion.

It is social convenience to use the 'I'. But this social convenience becomes truth, it becomes the center of your being, a false thing.

The 'I never existed, can never exist. But just because of social utility the child is trained, the consciousness becomes fixed around a center which is just utilitarian, not existential—and then you live in an illusion. And the whole life of a person who has not come to know that there is no ego, will be false, because it is based on a false foundation.

To be a witness means to drop the 'I'. The moment you can drop the 'I', immediately you become the witness. Then there is nothing else to do; you can only be the witness. This 'I' creates the problem. Hence he emphasis of all religious to become egoless, to be egoless, to be humble, not to be proud not to be conceited about it. Even if you have to use it, use it as a symbol. You have to use it, but use it knowingly—knowing that this is just a social convenience.

That attitude of non-attachment to the objects of desire in which the seeker knows that he is neither the doer nor the enjoyer, neither the restrained nor the restrainer, is called ordinary non-attachment.

When you become capable of remembering that you are the witness, this is the first stage of non-attachment.

He knows that whatever faces him in this life is the result of the deeds of his past life.

Try to see that whatsoever action is there, it is not arising out of you, but rather arising out of the chain of actions you have done in the past. Try to understand this distinction clearly. Whenever you do something, if somebody insults you, you think that the reaction is arising from you. That is wrong. It is arising not from you, but from the chain of your mind which has come from the past. You have been trained in the past that this is an insulting word.

I will tell you one anecdote. Kahlil Gibran writes somewhere that one man came to Lebanon. He was not a Lebanese, he didn't know the language of the country; he was totally a stranger. The moment he entered Lebanon he saw a very big palatial building, many people coming in and out, so he also entered to see what was going on there. It was a big hotel, but he thought, 'It seems the king has given a party—so many distinguished guests coming out, going in, and everybody is being served.' And, as the human mind works, he thought, 'It may be that because I have come to Lebanon, just for my reception, in my honour, the king is doing something.'

The moment he entered he was received by the manager, he was placed at a table, and food was served. He enjoyed it and he was very happy; he had never been so happy in his life. And then when he had finished his food, drink and everything, he started thanking them. But they could not understand his language, and he could not understand their language. They were placing a bill before him—it was a hotel—but he could not understand. He thought, 'They are giving in writing, "It was so good of you to accept the invitation. You have honoured us." So he took the bill, put it in his pocket, and thanked them again.

Then the manager became disturbed: either he was insane, because he was talking in such strange sounds they couldn't understand, or he was a rascal, just trying to deceive: so he was brought to the owner of the hotel. The man thought, "Now they are bringing me to the chief minister, or the prime minister of the country.' He again started thanking them. It was no use, so he was brought to the court.

When he entered the palatial building of the court, bigger than the hotel, he thought, 'Now this is the palace of the king, and he himself is going to receive me in person.' Again he started bowing down and thanking, and the magistrate thought, 'This man is either mad, or a perfect rascal,' so he punished him. And it was the punishment of that country in such cases that the man should be forced to sit on a donkey backwards, and a plaque should be hung around his neck on which it was written: 'This man has committed the crime of deception, and everybody should be aware.'

He was painted black, and he enjoyed it very much, because he thought, 'A strange country, with strange manners, but they are paying every attention to me. Naked he was placed on a donkey, a plaque was hung around his neck. He enjoyed it. Then the donkey started moving all over town, just to make the whole town aware that this man was a criminal. And a crowd, children and many cripples followed, and he enjoyed. He thought, 'These people are just following in my honour. 'The children were enjoying it, and he was also very happy and joyful, but only one sadness was in his heart: 'Nobody knows what is happening to me in my country. I wish they could become aware of how I have been received. And they will not believe me when I go back; they will say that I am just inventing stories.'

Then suddenly he saw a man in the crowd who belonged to his country. He was very happy and he said, 'Look ! How beautifully they have received me ! This is not only in my honour, but my country is honoured.' But the other man who knew the language of this country, Lebanon, simply disappeared in the crowd, hiding his face, because he knew what was happening. This was not an honour. And the man on the donkey thought, 'Jealousy, nothing else. This man is jealous. They have honoured me and they have not honoured him.'

You have a mind trained in many lives. Things come out of that, not out of you. You have a long chain of actions; whenever a new act is born in you, it comes out of that chain. It is a new link in that chain; it is born out of that chain, not out of you. When somebody insults you, you get angry. That anger comes from your past angers, not from you.

This difference has to be noted, because it will help you to become a witness. And that is what is meant by living moment to moment—that is the moment. Don't allow the chain of the past to react. Put aside the chain and let your consciousness function directly. Don't be influenced by the past; respond here and now, directly. The whole life will be different if you can act out of the present moment. But all your actions are almost always out of the past, never out of the present. And action that is born out of the present is non-binding; an action that is born out of the past chain is a new link in your bondage. But first one has to become aware.

When you get angry just look: from where is that anger coming ? from you or just from your past memories ? You have been insulted before, you have been angry before—that memory is there, waiting; that memory works like a wound. Again something happens and that memory starts functioning; that memory creates the same reaction again. If you watch and observe for twenty-four hours, you will see that you are just a mechanical robot: you are functioning out of memories, out of the past. The past is dead, and the dead is so weighty on you that your life is crushed under it. Look at the chain. This sutra says:

He Knows that whatever faces him in this life is the result of the deeds of his past life.

Not only that his reactions come from his past memories, but others' actions in connection with him are also part of his past actions. It happened, Buddha became enlightened and one of his cousins, Devadatta, tried to poison him, tried to kill him, in many ways tried to murder him. He was always a failure, fortunately. Somebody asked Buddha, 'Why don't you do something about it ? This man is constantly trying in many ways to kill you.' Once he brought a mad elephant and left the elephant near Buddha. The elephant was mad, in a rage. The elephant came running, but suddenly, just near Buddha, it stopped, bowed down, and closed it eyes as if it was meditating. So somebody asked, 'Why don't you do something about this man? And why is he doing such thing?

Buddha said, 'Because of my past actions. I must have hurt him in the past; he is simply reacting out of that chain. It is not his doing; I must have done some wrong to him in the past. And I must have done something good to this elephant in the past, otherwise there was no possibility. And I should remain now a witness. If I do something again in connection with Devadatta, then again a chain will be created. So let him be finished with my past deeds. But I am not going to create a new karma for the future.'

When someone insults you, the attitude of a witness of a person who is practising non-attachment, is this: 'I must have insulted him before, in some past life somewhere, because nothing is born without a cause. The cause must be there, this is only the effect. So I must wait and take it, accept is as part of my destiny and be finished with it, because if I do something again a new future is created and the chain continues.'

Someone insults you. If you answer in any way then the account is not closed, it remains open. If you don't respond then the account is closed. And this is the difference between the Eastern attitude and Christianity. Even very beautiful things sometimes can be basically wrong. Jesus says, 'If someone hits you on one cheek, give him the other.' This is a beautiful saying, and one of the most beautiful sayings ever uttered in the world.

But ask an Eastern Buddha. He will say, 'Don't do even that. When someone hits your cheek, remain as you were before he hit you. Don't change, don't do anything, because even giving him the other cheek is a response—a good response, a beautiful response, but a response—and you are creating karma again.'

Nietzsche somewhere criticizes Jesus for this. He says, 'If I hit Jesus' face on one cheek and he gives me the other, I will hit even harder on the other, because this man is insulting me, he is treating me like an insect. He is not giving me the same status as him.' Nietzsche says, ' It would be better if Jesus hits me back, because then he is behaving with me on equal terms. If he gives me the other cheek, he is trying to play the God, and he is insulting.'

That's possible. You can insult a person just by becoming superior. Not that Jesus means it, but you can do it. And just trying to become superior will be more insulting, and the other person will feel more hurt than if you had given him a good slap. The Eastern attitude is to not do anything in any way; to remain as if nothing has happened.

Somebody hits you: you remain as if nothing has happened. And this hit has come not from this person, but from your past deed. So accept it; it is your own doing. He has not done anything. And remain as if nothing has happened. Don't hit him back, and don't give him the other cheek because both will create a new chain. Be finished with it, so the account is closed with this man at least. And this way you close the accounts with all. ·

When all the accounts are closed you need not be reborn. This is the philosophy of going beyond life and death. Then you need not be reborn again; you simply disappear from this phenomenal world, from this bodily, physical world. Then you exist as cosmos, not as individual's. Jesus' saying is beautiful, very moral. But Buddha's attitude is spiritual, not only moral: not to do anything, because whatsoever you do creates future, and one has to stop creating future.

He knows whatever faces him in this life is the result of the deeds of his past life. Whether in pleasure or in pain, he can do nothing.

If you think you can do something, you can never become a witness; if you think you can do something, you will remain a doer. This has to be very deeply realized—that nothing can be done. Only then can the witness arise.

The life has to be observed, and if you observe life, you will come to feel that nothing can be done. Everything is happening. You are born: what have you done about it? It has not been any choice, you have not chosen to be born. You are black or white: you have not chosen to be black or white, it has happened. You are man or woman, intelligent or stupid: it has happened, you have not done anything about it. You will die, you will disappear from this body, you will be born in another. Look at all this as a happening, not as a doing on your part. If you feel that you are doing something, you can never become a witness.

The modern mind finds it very difficult to become a witness, because the modern mind thinks he can do something, the modern mind thinks he has willpower, the modern mind thinks that it is in his hands to change things and destiny. The modern mind goes on insisting to children, 'You are the master of your destiny.' This is foolish. You cannot do anything, and whenever you feel that you are doing something, you are under a wrong impression.

It happened once, under a tree many stones were piled. A building was soon going to be constructed, and those stones were piled there for that building, to be filled in the foundations. One small boy was passing, and as small boys are , he took a stone and threw it in the sky. The stone was rising upwards. It is very difficult for stones even to imagine that they can go upwards; they always go downwards. Just because of gravitation, stones always go downwards, they cannot go upwards. But every stone must be dreaming somehow or other to go upwards. In their dreams, stones must be flying, because dreams are fulfillments of those things which we cannot do. They are substitutes.

So all those stones must have dreamed somewhere, sometime, about flying. And this stone must have dreamed that someday he would fly, he would become a bird. And suddenly it happened. He was thrown, but he thought, 'I am rising.' He looked downwards. Other stones, his brothers and sisters, were lying down, so he said, 'Look! What are you doing there? Can't you fly? And I have done a miracle! I am flying, and I am going to the sky to see moons and stars!'

The other stones felt very jealous, but they couldn't do anything, so they thought, this stone must be unique, an avatar, a reincarnated superior being. We cannot fly. This stone must be a Krishna, a Buddha, a Christ. He has miraculous power; he is flying. And this is the greatest miracle for a stone.'

They felt jealous, they wept over their destiny, they were sad, but they couldn't do anything. Then they started feeling—because this is how mind goes on consoling—'Okay, you are one of us. You belong to us, to this pile, to this nation, to this race. We are happy that one of our brothers is flying.'

But then the moment came when the momentum of that small boy's throw was lost, the energy finished, and the stone started falling back. For a moment he felt dizzy, for a moment he felt, ' What is happening? And he couldn't control it. But suddenly, as everybody rationalizes, he rationalized, 'It is enough for the first day. I have gone too for, and I must go back now to my home.'

Then he thought, 'I am feeling homesick. It is better now to go back, to rest a little. I must go back to my brothers and sisters, to my community, and tell them what beautiful phenomena I have seen——the sky, infinite sky, and such vast space, stars, moons—so near. This has been a cosmic event, an historical event; it should be written for the generations to come, for them to remember that one of us had flown once into the sky, had become just like a bird. The dreams are fulfilled.'

He started falling back. When he came just near the pile he said, ' I am coming back. Don't look so sad. I will not leave you, I will never leave you. The world is beautiful, but nothing is like home.' He fell down.

And this is the story of your whole life. You are thrown; existence throws you. Then for certain moments you enjoy—life, flying, beauty, love, youth—but this is happening. It is happening just like breath coming in and going out. You are not doing anything; everything is a happening. Once you understand this, ego disappears, because ego exists only with the idea that you can do. To realize that nothing can be done is the highest point for the spiritual seeker to begin with, the climax of understanding. After that is transformation.

And if you cannot do anything, then when someone insults you, you can remain a witness because what can be done? You can look at what is happening, you can be detached. A pain comes, a suffering happens— what can you do? You can be witness. Pleasure comes, you are happy— what can you do? It has happened. It is happening just like night and day, morning and evening.

Watch your mind. There are moments of sadness, and immediately after them, moments of pleasure, then again moments of sadness. When you are sad, you are just on brink of being happy; when you are happy, you are just on the brink of being sad . And this goes on revolving. And you have not done anything really; you are just like that stone. He takes a happening for a doing that is fallacious. When you fall in love, what have you done? Can you do anything to fall in love? Can you fall in love consciously? Try it, and then you will see the impossibility: You cannot do anything. And if you have fallen in love, you cannot stop that falling. There are foolishnesses which belong to youth, and there are foolishnesses which belong to old age. This is the foolishness of the youth: he thinks, ' I am doing something when I am in love.' So he thinks, ' This is something of my doing.' It is a happening. And this is the foolishness of old age: old people go on saying, 'Don't fall in love. Stop yourself, control yourself—as if love can be controlled. But the whole society exists around the ego—control, doing, not happening. If you can look at life as a happening, whether in pleasure or in pain, he can do nothing. Indulgence is but a disease and affluence of all kinds a storehouse of adversity.

This is not condemnation; this is just giving you a hint that the opposite is hidden. When you are in pleasure, pain is there hidden, will come soon.

Indulgence is but a disease and affluence of all kinds a storehouse of adversity.

It is not a condemnation; this is simply the fact. But you go on forgetting. When you are happy, you forget that you were ever sad before; you forget that sadness will follow again. When you are sad, you forget that you were ever happy before, and you forget that happiness will follow again.

You are in a moving circle, in a moving wheel. That's why in the East, life is called a wheel, just a wheel moving every spoke will come up, and every spoke will go down and will again come up. You may not be able to connect—that's your misery. If you can connect, you can see.

Go into loneliness for at least twenty-one days and then watch. There is nobody who can make you happy or unhappy; there is nobody who can make you angry, pleased, or anything. You are alone there. Have a diary and watch and note down every mood that comes to you. Then for the first time you will become aware that there is no need for anybody to make you angry—you become angry by yourself. There is no need for anybody to make you sad—thee are moments when you suddenly feel sad. And thee is no need for anybody to make you happy—there are sudden glimpses when you are happy.

And if you can watch for twenty-one days and go on noting down, you will see a wheel emerging. And this wheel is so subtle; that's why you are not aware and you never connect it. If you watch deeply, you can even say that one mood is passing, and you can say what will follow, which spoke is going to come. If you have observed basically, deeply, you can predict your moods. Then you can say, 'On Monday morning I will be angry.'

Much research is going on in Soviet Russia about moods. And they say a calendar can be made for every person: on Mondays he will be angry; on Saturdays, in the morning he will be happy; on Tuesdays, in the evening, he will feel sexual. If you observe yourself, you can also approximately fix a routine, a wheel, of your life. And then many things become possible. Russian psychologists have suggested that if this can be done—and this can be done—then family life will become more easy, because you can look at your wife's calendar, and your wife can look at your calendar. Then there is no need to get angry about anything; this is how things are going to happen.

You know that on Tuesdays the wife is going to be terrible, so you accept it. You know from the very beginning that it is going to be on that day, so from the morning you can remain a witness, you need not get involved in it; it is your wife's inner work. Two beings moving side by side need not get concerned with the other's spokes. And when she is unhappy, sad, it is just foolish to get angry about it, because you create more sadness through it. The day when your wife is unhappy, it is better to help her in every way, because she is ill. It is just like menses, a periodical thing.

Now in Czechoslovakia, one research has proved that not only women have their menses, periods, but men also; every twenty-eight days they become depressed for three or four days. And it should be so, because man cannot be anything else than a wheel; if woman is a wheel, man must be a wheel. And there are some secretions in the blood in man also: every twenty-eight days, after four weeks, they pass through a menstrual period. For four or five days they are sad. (Check tape for last 2 sentences)

With every menses, every woman becomes depressed, violent, angry, and her intelligence goes low. It is now a proven fact that girls in menses should not go to sit for examinations, because they unnecessarily lose much. Their IQ is low when they are in menses, and unnecessarily they lose much. They should not be forced to go to the examination when they are having a period; they cannot compete rightly. They are angry, disturbed, the whole system is a chaos inside. But there is no rule yet.

In the East it has been one of the traditions that whenever a woman is in her period, she should not make any contact with anybody. She should move into a lonely room and remain closed and meditating for four days, because if she is out mixing with people, she will create unnecessary bad karmas, and they will create chains. She should not touch food, because she is in such a chaos, the food becomes poisonous.

Now scientifically also it is proved that when a woman is in menses, if she takes a flower in her hand, the flower immediately goes sad. Subtle vibrations, chaotic vibrations, affect it. A woman in menses should not be in contact with people; it is better if she simply meditates and rests. But such periods are with men also. They are more subtle. The body secretes some hormones in the bloodstream.

This calendar can be maintained. You can observe your life for two or three months, impartially, and then you can know that you are moving in a wheel, and others are only excuses; you impose upon them. You get sad when you are alone also, but if you are with someone you think the other is making you sad. And man and woman are not different, cannot be. They are not two different species, they are one species, and everything has a positive-negative relationship. Man ejaculates in intercourse; women don't ejaculate, but a subtle ejaculation happens in bloodstream, because women are passive. But as far as childbirth is concerned, they are positive, and man is passive. That's why menses with woman is positive—ejaculation happens, blood comes out of the body. In man, ejaculation happens, but it moves into the bloodstream; hormones are released. Man is born out of man and woman; woman is born out of man and woman—in every individual both are there.

I remember, once Mulla Nasrudin's wife said to him, 'Nasrudin, I wonder. Sometimes I get very puzzled. Sometimes you look so manly, so powerful and strong, and sometimes so effeminate, so feminine. What is the matter?' So Nasrudin brooded, contemplated, and then he said, 'It must be hereditary, because half of my parents were men, and half of my parents were women.

But everyone is bi-sexual; no one belongs to one sex, and cannot belong to one sex. Half of you is man, and half of you is woman. So the difference is only of which part is visible. You may be man only because the male part is visible on the surface, and the female part is hidden behind. You are a woman if the female part is visible on the surface, and the male part is hidden behind.

That's why if a woman get ferocious, she will be more ferocious than a man, because then, she simply comes out of her surface, and the hidden is man. Ordinarily when a woman is angry, she is not so angry as man, not so aggressive as man, but if she is really angry then man is nothing before her. A man can be more loving than a woman. He is not ordinarily so, but if he is then no woman can be compared with him, because then the hidden part comes out. And man has not used the hidden part; it is fresh, alive—more alive than woman. So if a man is really in love, he is more loving than any woman, because then his hidden woman which is fresh, unused, comes out. And when a woman is angry, filled with hatred, no man is a comparison, because the hidden, fresh aggression comes out.

And this happens in life: as people grow old, men become more effeminate, and women become more manly. That's why old women are very dangerous. The stories about mother-in-laws are not just inventions. They are dangerous, because now the female part has been used so much that it has dissipated, and the male part has come in. Sometimes woman may grow moustaches when they are old. Their voice will become manly; it will not be so feminine, fine it will become coarse. Because one part has been used. And by the time menopause happens, when the menses have stopped, the female part is dropping, the surface is dropping, and the inner part is working more and more. Old men become effeminate; their coarseness is lost. So this is a rare phenomenon: if they have really live silently, beautifully, then old men become more beautiful than old women. When young, a woman is just wonderful, very beautiful;

everything, every curve of her being is beautiful. Old woman become coarse, the beauty is lost. Old men become more beautiful than they were when they were young. Look at Mahatma Gandhi's pictures. When he was young, he was ugly. The older he grows, the more beautiful. Only when he was in his last stage of life was he beautiful. This happens because man becomes more effeminate; more curves come into his being and corners become soft. This is not to condemn.

Every union leads inevitably to separation.

Every union leads to separation; every marriage is a preparation for divorce.

The ignorant suffer the maladies of mental anxiety.

The ignorant suffer because of ignorance; because they cannot see this polarity. If they can see that every union is going to become a separation , they will neither be happy about the union nor unhappy about the separation. And if you are not happy about the marriage and not happy about the divorce, you have transcended both. Then a relationship grows which cannot be called marriage and cannot be called divorce. That relationship can be eternal. But marriage implies divorce, union implies separation; birth implies death. So be aware of the opposite, that will help you to become a witness. It will lessen your happiness, it will lessen your misery also. And a moment will come when happiness and misery will become the same. When they become the same, you have transcended.

And this is the way they can become the same: when happiness comes, search for the hidden unhappiness somewhere in it—you will find it. When unhappiness comes, search for the happiness hiding somewhere— you will find it. And then you know what happiness and unhappiness are not two things, but two aspects of the same coin. And don't believe too much in the aspect that is visible, because the invisible will become visible. It is only a question of time.

All material things are perishable, because time is constantly devouring them. Through the understanding of scriptural precepts, one's faith in material things is uprooted and one's mind freed of them. This is called ordinary non-attachment.

This is through effort, understanding. With mind you can achieve this ordinary non-attachment. But this is not the goal; this is just the beginning.

When thoughts like: I am not the doer, my past deeds are the doers, or God himself is the doer....'

Even such thoughts drop. These were the base of the first; these thoughts were the base of the ordinary non-attachment. When even they

cease to worry the seeker, a stage of silence, equilibrium and peace is attained. This is called sublime non-attachment.

Because to constantly think that, 'I am not the doer,' shows that you believe you are the doer, otherwise why go on constantly saying that I am not the doer? Once it happened, one Hindu sannyasin, a traditional monk, stayed with me for a few days. Every day in the morning he would sit in the Brahmamuhurat, just before the sunrise, and repeat constantly, 'I am not the body. I am the soul supreme. I am not the body.'

So I heard him doing it, saying that for many days, and then I said, 'If really you know that you are not the body, why repeat it? If you really know you are the supreme self, then who are you convincing every morning? That shows you don't know. You are just trying to convince yourself that you are not the body, but you know you are the body. That's why the need to convince.'

Remember this , the mind works in this way; whenever you try to convince yourself of something, the contrary is the case. If a person tries too much to say, 'I love you,' know will that something is wrong. If a person tries to say too much about anything, that shows that the contrary exists within-he is trying to convince himself, not you. Whenever a husband feels guilty that he has looked at another woman, or has been friendly, or was attracted, then he comes home and that day he will be more loving to the wife. He will bring ice-cream or something. So whenever the husband brings ice-cream, beware—because now he is not trying to convince you, he is trying to convince himself that he loves his wife more than anybody else.

Whenever mind becomes aware that something has gone wrong, that wrong has to be put right. The first effort for non-attachment is such effort. You go on insisting to yourself, 'I am not the body. I am not the doer,' but you know well that you are the doer, you are the body. But this will help. One day you will become aware of both these polarities: that you are insisting that you are not, and still you believe that you are the body. Then both drop: you simply remain silent, you don't say anything. Neither you say, 'I am the doer,' Nor you say, ' I am the witness.' You simply drop this whole nonsense. You allow things as they are. You don't say anything you don't make any statement. Then silence, equilibrium, and peace are attained—when you don't make any statement.

Somebody asked Buddha, 'Are you the body? Or are you the soul?' Buddha remained silent. The man insisted Buddha said, 'Don't force me, because whatsoever statement I make will be wrong. If I say I am the body, it is wrong, because I am not. If I say I am not the body, that too shows that somehow I am attached to the body, otherwise why this denial? Why this botheration to say that I am no the body? So I will not make any statement. If you can understand, look at me, at what I am.'

When you simply are—without any statement, without any idea, without any theory, without any concept; when you simply are, when you have become a tree, a rock, you exist, that's all. And you allow existence to flow from you, within you. You don't create any resistance, you don't say, 'I am this,' because every statement will be a definition, and every statement will make you finite.

But this will not happen immediately and directly, remember. You cannot drop unless you have made the first effort. So first try, ' I am the witness.' And bring it to such intensity that in that intensity you become aware that even this is futile. Then drop it, and be yourself.

It happened once, Mulla Nasrudin went to England. His English was not very good, just like me. That is not much. He has a very beautiful dog, but very ferocious. So he put a plaque on the door. Instead of writing 'Beware of the dog', he wrote 'Be aware of the dog'. That is wrong English—but wrongly he did a right thing, because the whole emphasis is changed. When you say 'Be aware of the dog', emphasis is on the dog. When you say 'Be aware of the dog', the emphasis on you. And this English word 'beware' is beautiful. Make it two: be plus aware.

Be plus aware is the first step. In the second step, awareness also has disappeared. Simply be. Don't be even aware because that will create an effort. Simply be. When you are in that state of being, not doing anything, not even witnessing, because that too is a subtle doing.

a state of silence, equilibrium, and peace is attained. This is called sublime non-attachment.

•••

2

ONE IN THE MANY

If everything is simply happening, then can there be any ultimate purpose to it all, or is life just an accident? Can it be said that life is evolving towards some ultimate goal?

It is very difficult, particularly for the Western mind, to understand that life is purposeless. And it is beautiful that it is purposeless. If it is purposeful then the whole thing become absurd—then who will decide the purpose? Then some God has to be conceived who decides the purpose, and then human beings become just puppets, then no freedom is possible. And if there is some purpose then life becomes businesslike; it cannot be ecstatic. The West has been thinking in terms of purpose, but the East has been thinking in terms of purposelessness. The East says life is not a business, it is a play. And a play has no purpose really; it is non-purposeful. Or, you can say play is its own purpose; to play is enough. Life is not reaching towards some goal; life itself is the goal. It is not evolving towards some ultimate; this very moment, here and now, life is ultimate, life as it is accepted in the East. It is not moving towards some end, because if there is some end, who will decide the end and why? If God decides it, then you can ask the same question about God: 'What is the purpose of creating a world with purpose? Or, 'Why should he create a purposive world?' Or even more deeply, 'What is the purpose of God's existence?'

Maybe life has a purpose and God decides the purpose, but then God's existence has to be questioned, why he exists, and that way the question is simply pushed one step ahead. Then God becomes purposeless, or you have to create another God to decide the purpose of this God. Then you will be a regress ad infinitum; then there is no end to it. Somewhere deep, you will have to come to the conclusion that this phenomenon is purposeless, otherwise there is no end.

So why go from the world to the God? Why not say the life itself is purposeless? The whole game of logicians, theologicians, is stupid in a way. They say, 'God created the world, because how could the world come into existence if there was no one who created it?' But the question can be asked, 'Who created the god?'—and then they fall on their own. They say, 'God is uncreated.' If god can exist without being created, why can't this life itself exist without being created? If you accept that something is possible without being created, then what is the trouble? Then why think about a God who created the world?

The East says God is not the creator, God is the creation. Nobody has created it; it is there. It has been so always, it will be so always—sometimes manifest, sometimes unmanifest; sometimes visible, sometime invisible. It goes on moving in a periodical rhythm, in a circle. But existence itself is uncreated and it has no goal.

Then think about it in other ways also. Firstly: if there is a goal, why hasn't it been achieved yet? The existence has been existing timelessly; millions and millions of light-years it has existed, and the goal has not been reached yet. When will it be reached? If so many millions and millions of light-years have passed and the goal is nowhere to be seen, when will it be reached? Secondly: if some day the goal is reached, what will happen to existence? Will it disappear? When the purpose is fulfilled, then what? Conceive a moment somewhere is the future when the purpose is fulfilled. Then for what will existence exist then? Then it will be purposeless for it to exit.

The reality is this: that it is already always purposeless. There is no goal towards which the existence is moving. It is moving, but not towards any goal. It has a value, but the value is not in the end, the value is intrinsic.

You love someone. Have you asked the question, 'For what purpose does love exit? The mind, a calculating mind, is bound to ask, 'Why love? What is the purpose? If you can answer then one thing is certain— that you are not in love. If you can show the purpose, then love is not there; it is a business, it is bargain. But lovers will always say there is no purpose to it. To be in love is the goal. The goal is not somewhere else; it is intrinsic, it is in the very phenomenon of love. The goal is already achieved. When you are happy, have you asked, 'What is the purpose of being happy? Can there be any purpose of being happy? When you are happy you never ask, because the question is absurd. Happiness is itself the goal; there is no purpose to it.

Life is like love, life is like happiness. Life is existence—no goal. And once you can understand this, your ways of living will change totally, because if there is no purpose in life itself, there is no need to create a purpose for your individual life also—no need. Because of individual purposes you become tense; something has to be achieved. Then an achieving mind is created which is always trying to achieve something or other. And whenever something is achieved, again the mind ask, 'Now what? What is to be achieved now?' It cannot remain with itself, it has to go on achieving. This achieving mind will never be blissful; it will be always tense. And whenever something is achieved the achieving mind will feel frustrated, because now new goals have to be invented. This is happening in America. Many of the goals of the past century have been achieved, so America is in a deep frustration. All the goals of the founding fathers who created America and the American Constitution, are almost achieved. In America, the society has become affluent for the first time in the whole history of mankind. Almost everybody is rich. The poor man in America is a rich man here in India.

The goals have almost have been achieved. Now what to do? Society has become affluent: food is there, shelter is there, everybody has got a car, radio, refrigerator, TV—now what to do? A deep frustration is felt; some other goals are needed. And there seem to be no goals. Instead of one car you can have two cars—two car garage has become the goal. Or you can have two houses. But that will be achieved within ten years. Whatsoever the goal, it can be achieved. Then the achieving mind feels frustrated. What to do now? It needs again a goal, and you have to invent a goal.

So the whole American business now depends on inventing goals. Give people goals—that's what advertisements and the whole business of advertising is doing. Create goals, seduce people—'Now this is the goal! You must have this, otherwise life is purposeless!' They start running, because they have an achieving mind. But where does it lead? It leads into more and more neurosis.

Only a non-achieving mind can be at peace. But a non-achieving mind is possible only in the background of a cosmic purposelessness. If the whole existence is purposeless, then there is no need for you to be purposeful. Then you can play, you can sing and dance, you can enjoy, you can love and live, and there is no need to create any goal. Here and now, this very moment, the ultimate is present. If you are available, the ultimate can enter in you. But you are not available here. Your mind is somewhere in the future, in some goal.

Life has got no purpose and this is the beauty of it. If there was some purpose, life would have been mean—just futile. It is not a business, it is a play. In India we have been calling it leela; leela means a cosmic play. The God is as if playing—energy overflowing. Not for some purpose, just enjoying itself, just a small child playing. For what purpose? Running after butterflies, collecting coloured stones on the beach, dancing under the sun, running under the trees, collecting flowers for what purpose? Ask a child. He will look at you as if you are a fool. There is no need for purpose.

Your mind has been corrupted. Universities, colleges, education, society, have corrupted you. They have made it a conditioning deep down within you, that unless something has a purpose deep down within you, that unless something has a purpose, it is useless—so everything must have a purpose. A child playing has no purpose. At the most, if the child could explain, he would say, 'Because I feel good Running, I feel more alive, Collecting flowers, I enjoy, it is ecstatic.' But there is no purpose. The very act in itself is beautiful ecstatic. To be alive is enough, there is no need for any purpose.

Why ask for anything else? Can't you be satisfied just by being alive? It is such a phenomenon. Just think of yourself being a stone. You could have been, because many are still stones. You must have been somewhere in the past, sometime a stone. Think of yourself being a tree. You must have been somewhere a tree, a bird, an animal, an insect. And then think of yourself being a man-conscious, alert, the peak, the climax of all possibilities. And you are not content with it. You need a purpose, otherwise life is useless.

Your mind has been corrupted by economists, mathematicians, theologians. They have corrupted your mind, because they all talk about purpose. They say, 'Do something if something is achieved through it. Don't do anything which leads nowhere.' But I tell you, that the more you can enjoy things which are useless, the happier you will be. The more you can enjoy things which are purposeless, the more innocent and blissful you will be.

When you don't need any purpose, you simply celebrate your being. Just that you are, you feel gratitude; just that you breathe. It is such a blessing that you can breathe, that you are alert, conscious live, aflame. Is it not enough? You need something to achieve and then only you can feel good? Then you can feel valued; then you can feel life is justified? What more can you achieve than what you are? What more can be added to your life? What more can you add to it? Nothing can be added, and the effort will destroy you—the effort to add something.

But for many centuries all over the world, they have been teaching every child to be purposive. 'Don't waste your time! Don't waste your life!' And what do they mean? They mean, 'Transform your life into a bank balance. When you die, you must die rich. That is the purpose.'

Here, in the East—particularly the mystics we are talking about, the Upanishads—they say, 'Live richly.' In the West they say, 'Die a rich man.' And these are totally different things. If you want to live richly, you have to live here and now; not a single moment is to be lost. If you want to achieve something, you will die a rich man. But you will live a poor man; your life will be poor.

Look at rich people. Their life is absolutely poor, because they are wasting their life: transforming their life into bank balances, changing their life into money, into big houses, big cars. Their whole effort is that life has to be changed for some things. When they die, you can count their things.

Buddha became a beggar. He was born a king, he became a beggar. Why? Just to live richly. Because he came to understand that there are two ways to live: one is to die richly, another is to live richly. And any man who has any understanding will choose to live richly, because dying a rich man doesn't mean anything; you simply wasted yourself for nothing. But this is possible only if you can conceive that the whole existence is purposeless; it is a cosmic play. A continuous beautiful game, a beautiful hide-and-seek-not leading anywhere, nowhere is the goal.

If this is the background, then you need not be worried about individual purposes, evolution, progress. This word 'progress' is the basic disease of the modern age. What is the need? All that can be enjoyed is available; all that you need to be happy is here and now. But you create conditions, and you say that unless these conditions are fulfilled you cannot be happy. You say, 'These conditions must be fulfilled first: this type of house, this type of clothes, this type of car, this type of wife, this type of husband. All these conditions have to be fulfilled first, then I can be happy.

As if by being happy you are going to oblige the whole universe. And who is going to fulfill your conditions? Who is worried? But you will try for those conditions. And the effort is going to be so long that they can never be fulfilled really, because whenever something is fulfilled, by the time it is fulfilled, the goal has shifted.

One of my friends was contesting an election, political election, so he came to me for blessing. I said, 'I will not give the blessing, because I am not your enemy, I am a friend. I can only bless that you must not get elected, because that will be first step towards madness.' But he wouldn't listen to me. He was elected, he became a member. Next year he came again for my blessing and he said, 'Now I am trying to be a deputy minister.'

I asked him, 'You were saying that if you could become a member of parliament you would be very happy, but I don't see that you are happy. You are more depressed and more sad than you ever were before.'

He said, 'Now only this is the problem. I am worried. There is much competition. Only if I can become deputy minister will everything be okay.'

He became a deputy minister. When I was passing through the capital, he came to see me again and he said, 'I think you were right, because now the problem is how to become the minister. And I think this is the goal. I am not going to change it. Once I become the minister, it is finished.'

He has become the minister now, and he came to me a few days ago and he said, 'Just one blessing more. I must become chief minister.' And he is getting more and more worried, more and more puzzled, because more problems have to be faced, more competition, more ugly politics. And he is a good man, not a bad man.

I told him, 'Unless you become the supreme most God, you are not going to be satisfied.' But he cannot look back and cannot understand the logic of the mind, the logic of the achieving mind. It can never be satisfied; the way it behaves creates more and more discontent. The more you have, the more discontent you will feel, because more arenas become open for you in which to compete, to achieve. A poor man is more satisfied, because he cannot think that he can achieve much. Once he starts achieving something, he thinks more is possible. The more you achieve, the more becomes possible, and it goes on and on forever.

A meditator needs a non-achieving mind, but a nonachieving mind is possible only if you can be content with purposelessness. Just try to understand the whole cosmic play and be a part in it. Don't be serious, because a play can never be serious. And even if the play needs you to be serious, be playfully serious, don't be really serious. Then this very moment becomes rich. Then this very moment you can move into the ultimate.

The ultimate is not in the future; it is in the present, hidden here and now. So don't ask about purpose—there is none. And I say it is beautiful that there is none. If there was purpose then your God would be just a managing director, or a big business man, an industrialist; or something like that.

Jesus says—somebody asked him, 'Who will be capable to enter into a kingdom of your God? Jesus said, 'Those who are like small children.' This is the secret. What is the meaning of being a small child? The meaning is that the child is never businesslike, he is always playful.

If you can become playful you have become a child again, and only children can enter into the kingdom of God, nobody else. Because children can play without asking where it is leading. They can make houses of sand without asking whether they are going to be permanent. Can somebody live in them? Will they be able to resist the wind that is blowing? They know that within minutes they will disappear. But they are very serious when they are playing. They can even fight for their sand houses, or houses of cards. They are very serious when they are creating. They are enjoying. And they are not fools: they know that these houses are just card houses and everything is make-believe. Why waste time in thinking in terms of business? Why not live more and more playfully, non-seriously, ecstatically? Ecstasy is not something which you can achieve by some efforts: ecstasy is a way of living. Moment to moment you have to be ecstatic; simple things have to be enjoyed. And life gives millions of opportunities to enjoy. You will miss them if you are purposive.

If you are not purposive, every moment you will have so many opportunities to be ecstatic. A flower, lonely flower in the garden—you can dance if you are non-purposive. The first star in the evening—you can sing if you are non-purposive. A beautiful face—you can see the divine in it if you are non-purposive. All around divine is happening, ultimate is showering. But you will be able to see it only if you are non-purposive and playful.

It is felt by many, in the West and elsewhere, that the peak of love is reached only between an 'I' and a 'thou' If I and thou are both dropped, can love still exist?

Can love exist without relationship?

Love, life, light—these three l's are the most mysterious. And the mystery is this—that you cannot understand them logically. If you are illogical you can penetrate them; if you are simply logical you cannot understand, because the whole phenomenon depends on a paradox. Try to understand.

When you love someone, two are needed: I and thou. Without two, how can love be possible? If you are alone, how can you relate, how can you love? If you are alone, there can be no love, love is possible only when there are two; this is the base. But if they remain two, love is again impossible. If they continue to be two, then again love is impossible. Two are needed for love to exist, and then there is a second need-that the two must merge and become one. This is the paradox.

'I' and 'thou' is a basic requirement for love to exist, but this is only the base. The temple can come only when these two merge into one. And the mystery is that somehow you remain two, and somehow you become one. This is illogical. Two lovers are two, and still one. They have found a bridge somewhere where 'I' disappears, 'thou' disappears; where a unity is formed, a harmony comes into being. Two are needed to create that harmony, but two are needed to dissolve into it.

It is just like this. A river flows; two banks are needed. A river cannot flow with only one bank. It is impossible; the river cannot exist. Two banks are needed for the river to flow. But if you look a little deeper, those two banks are joined together just below the river. If they are not joined, then also the river cannot exist; it will simply drop into the abyss. Two banks, apparently two on the surface, are on deep down.

Love exists like a river between two persons who on the surface remain two, but deep down have become one. That's why I say it is paradoxical. Two are needed just to be dissolve into one. So love is a deep alchemy, and very delicate. If you really become one, love will disappear, the river cannot flow. If you really remain two, love will disappear, because there can be no river in an abyss, if the two banks are really separate. So lovers create a game in which on the surface they remain two, and deep down they become one.

Sometimes they fight also; sometimes they are angry also; sometimes in every way they separate—but this is only on the surface. Their separation is just to get married again; their fight is just to create love again. They go a little away from each other just to come and meet again, and the meeting after the separation is beautiful. They fight to love again. They are intimate enemies. Their enmity is a play, they enjoy it.

If there is really love, you can enjoy the fight. If there is no love, only then the fight becomes a problem. Otherwise you can enjoy, it is a game. It creates hunger. If you have ever loved, then you know that love always reaches peaks after you have been fighting. Fight—you create the separation. And with separation the hunger arises, you feel starved. The other is needed more. You fall in love again. Then there is a more intense meeting.

To create that intensity the two should remain two, and at the same time, simultaneously, they should become one.

In India, we have pictured Shiva as Ardhnarishwar—half-man, half-woman. That is the only symbol of its type all over the world. Shiva—half is man, half is woman; half Shiva and half Parvati, his consort. Half the body is of man and half of woman: Ardhanarishvar, halfman, half-woman. That is the symbol. Lovers join together, but on the surface they remain two. Shiva is one, the body is two—half comes from Parvati, half he contributes. The body is two, on the surface the banks are two; in the depth the souls have mingled and become one.

Or, look at it in this way. The room is dark. You bring two lamps into it, two candles into it. Those two candles remain two, but their light has mingled and become one. You cannot separate the light. You cannot say, 'This light belongs to this candle, and that light belongs to that candle.' Light has mingled and become one. The spirit is like light. The body is the candle.

Two lovers are only two bodies, but not two souls. This is very difficult to achieve. That's why love is one of the most difficult things to achieve, and if even for moments you can achieve, it is worth it. If even only for moments in your whole life, if even for moments in your whole life, if even for moments you can achieve this oneness with someone, this oneness will become the door for the diving. Love achieved becomes the door for the divine, because then you can feel how this universe exists in the many and remains one.

But this can come only through experience——if you love a person and you feel that you are two and still one. And this should not be just a thought, but an experience. You can think, but thinking is of no use. This must be an experience: how the bodies have remained two and the inner beings have merged, melted into each other——the light has become one.

Once experienced, then the whole philosophy of the Upanishads becomes exactly clear, absolutely clear. These many are just the surface: behind each individual is hidden the non-individual, behind each part is hidden the whole. And if two can exist as two on the surface, why not many? If two can remain two and still one, why can't many remain many and still one? One in the many is the message of the Upanishads. And this will remain only theoretical if you have never been in love.

But people go on confusing love with sex. Sex may be part of love, but sex is not love. Sex is just a physical, biological attraction, and in sex you remain two. In sex you are concerned with the other, you are concerned with yourself. You are simply exploiting the other; you are simply using the other for some biological satisfaction of your own, and the other is using you. That's why sexual partners never feel any deep intimacy. They are using the other; the other is not a person. The other is not a thou; the other is just an it, a thing you can use, and the other is using you. Deep down it is mutual masturbation and nothing else.. The other is used as a device. It is not love, because you don't care for the other.

Love is totally different. It is not using the other; it is caring for the other. It is just being happy in the other. It is not your happiness that you derive from the other: if the other is happy, you are happy, and the other's happiness becomes your happiness. If the other is healthy, you feel healthy. If other is dancing, you feel a dance inside. If the other is smiling, the smile penetrates you and becomes your smile.

Love is the happiness of the other; sex is happiness of your own, the other has to be used. In love the other's happiness has become even more significant than your own. Lover's are each other's servants; sex partners are each other's exploiters.

Sex can exist in the milieu of love, but then it has a different quality; it is not sexual at all. Then it is one of the many ways of merging into each other. One of the many—not the only, not the sole, not the supreme. Many are the ways to merge into each other. Two lovers can sit silently with each other, and the silence can become the merger. Really only lovers can sit silently.

Wives and husbands cannot sit silently, because silence becomes boredom. So they go on talking about something or other. Even nonsense, rubbish, rot, they go on talking just to avoid the other. Their talk is to avoid the other, because if there is not talk the other's presence will be felt, and the other's presence is boredom. They are bored with each other, so they go on talking. They go on giving each other news of the neighbourhood, what was in the newspaper, what was on radio, what was on the TV, and what was in the film. They go on talking and chattering just to create a screen, a smoke-screen, so the other is not felt. Lovers never like to chatter. Whenever lovers are together they will remain silent, because in silence, merging is possible.

Lovers can merge in many ways. Both can enjoy a certain thing, and that enjoyment becomes a merger. Two lovers can meditate on a flower and enjoy the flower—then the flower becomes the merger. Both enjoying the same thing, both feeling ecstatic about the same thing, they merge. Sex is only one of the ways. Two lovers can enjoy poetry, a haiku, two lovers can enjoy painting, two loves can just go for a walk and enjoy the walk together. The only thing necessary is togetherness. Whatsoever the act, if they can be together, they can merge.

Sex is the one of the ways of being together, bodily together. And I say not the supreme, because it depends. If you are a very gross person, then sex seems to be the supreme. If you are a refined person, if you have a high intelligence, then in anything you can merge. If you know higher realms of happiness, simply listening to music you can move in a deeper ecstasy than sex. Or simply sitting near a waterfall and the sound of the waterfall, and in that sound you both can merge. You are no more there— only the water falling and the sound—and that can become a higher peak of orgasm than can ever be attained through sex. Sex is for the gross. That is only one of the many ways in which lovers can merge and forget their I and thou and become one.

And unless you transcend sex and find out other ways, sooner or later you will be fed-up with your lover, because sex will become repetitive, it will become mechanical. And then you will start looking for another partner, because the new attracts. Unless your partner remains constantly new you will get fed-up. And it is very difficult: if you have only one way of enjoying each other's togetherness, it is bound to become a routine. If you have so many ways to be together, only then can your togetherness remain fresh, alive, young and always new.

Lovers are never old. Husbands and wives are always old. They may be married only for one day, but they are old—one day old. The mystery has gone, the newness disappeared. Lovers are always young. They may have been together for seventy years but they are still young, the freshness is there. And this is possible only if sex is one of the ways of being together, not the only way. Then you can find millions of ways of being together, and you enjoy that togetherness. That togetherness is felt as oneness.

If two can exist as one, then many can exist as one. Love becomes the door for meditation, prayer. That is the meaning when Jesus goes on insisting that love is God—because love becomes the door, the opening, towards the divine.

So, to conclude: love is a relationship and yet not a relationship. Love exists between two, that's why you can call it a relationship. And still, if love exists at all it is not a relationship, because the two must disappear and become one. Hence I call it one of the basic paradoxes, one of the basic mysteries which logic cannot reveal.

If you ask logic and mathematics, they will say that if there are two, they will remain two, then they cannot become one. If they become one, then they cannot remain two. This is simple Aristotlean logic: one is one, two are two and if you say that two have become one, then they cannot remain two. And this is the problem—that love is both two and one simultaneously. If you are too much logic-obsessed, love is not for you.

But even an Aristotle falls in love, because logic is one thing, but nobody is ready to lose love for logic. Even Aristotle falls in love, and even an Aristotle knows that there are points where mathematics is transcended—two become one and yet remain two.

This has been one of the problems for theologicians all over the world, and they have discussed if for many centuries. No conclusion, has been reached, because no conclusion can be reached through logic . Not only with lovers—the same is the problem with God. Whether the devotee becomes one or remains separate—the same problem. A bhkta, a devotee—whether he remains ultimately separate from his God or becomes one-the same problem.

Mohammedans insist that he remains separate, because if he becomes one then love cannot exist. When you have become one, who is going to love and whom? So Mohammedans pray, ' let me be separate so that I can love you. Let there be a gap so that devotees can be in prayer and love.' Hindus have said that the devotees becomes one with the divine. But then it's a problem: If the devotees becomes one with the divine, then where is the devotion? Where can the devotion exist? And if the devotee becomes the divine he becomes equal, so God is not higher than the devotee.

My attitude is this: Just as it happens in love, it happens with the divine. You remain separate and yet you; become one. You remain separate on the surface; in the depths you have become one. The devotees becomes the God, and still remains the devotees. But then it is illogical. You can refute me very easily, you can argue against it very easily. But if you have loved, you will understand.

And if you have not loved yet then don't waste a single moment—be in love immediately! Because life cannot give you a higher peak than love. And if you cannot achieve a natural peak that life offers to you, you cannot be capable, worthy, to achieve any other peaks which are not ordinarily available. Meditation is a higher peak than love. If you cannot love, are incapable of love, meditation is not for you.

It happened once, a man came to Ramanuja. Ramanuja was a mystic, a devotee mystic, a very unique person—a philosopher and yet a lover, a devotee. It rarely happens – a very acute mind, a very penetrating mind, but with a very overflowing heart. A man came and asked Ramanuja, 'Show me the way towards the divine. How can I attain the God?

So Ramanuja asked, 'First let me ask a question. Have you loved anybody ever?

The devotee must have been a really religious person. He said, 'what are you talking about? Love? I am a celibate. I avoid woman just as one should avoid diseases. I don't look at them. I close my eyes.'

Ramanuja said, 'Still, think a little. Move into the past. Find out. Somewhere in your heart, has ever there been any flickering, any, even a small one, of love?

The man said, 'But I have come here to learn prayer, not to learn love. Teach me how to pray. And you are talking about worldly things. And I have heard that you are a great mystic saint, and I have come here just to be led into the divine, not to talk about worldly things!'

Ramanuja is reported to have said...even he become very sad, and said to the man, 'Then I cannot help you. If you have no experience of love, then there is no possibility for any experience of prayer. So first go into the world and love. And when you have loved and you are enriched through it, then come to me. Because only a lover can understand what prayer is. If you don't know anything illogical through experience, you cannot understand. And love is prayer given by nature easily—you cannot attain even that. Prayer is love not given so easily. It is achieved only when you reach higher peaks of totality. Much effort is needed to achieve it. For love, no effort is needed; it is available, it is flowing. You are resisting it.'

The same is the problem. And the problem arises because of our logical minds. Aristotale says, 'A is A, B is B, and A cannot be B.' This is a simple logical process. If you ask the mystics, they say, ' A is A, B is B, but A also can be B, and B also can be A.' Life is not divide into solid blocks. Life is a flow; it transcends blocks. It moves from one pole to the other. Love is a relationship, and yet not a relationship.

Can one be absorbed in doing something—for. instance, these dynamic meditation techniques—with absolute total intensity, and at the same time remain a witness who is separate, apart?

The same is the problem in many forms. You think that a witness is something apart, separate. It is not. Your intensity, your wholeness, is your witness. So when you are witnessing and doing something, you are not two—the doer is the witness.

For example, you are dancing here in kirtan. You are dancing: the dancer and the witness are not two, there is no separation. the separation is only in language. The dancer is the witness. And if the dancer is not the witness then you cannot be total in the dance, because the witness will need some energy and you will have to divide yourself. A part will remain a witness, and the remaining will move in the dance. It cannot be total; it will be divided. And this is not what is meant, because really this is the state of a schizophrenic patient—divided, split. It is pathological. If you become two, you are ill. You must remain one. You must move totally into the dance, and your totality will become the witness. It is not going to be a part set apart: your wholeness is aware. This happens.

So don't try to divide yourself. While dancing, become the dance. Just remain alert: don't fall asleep, don't be unconscious. You are not under a drug; you are alert, fully alert. But this alertness is not a part standing aloof; it is your totality, it is your whole being.

But this again the same thing as whether two lovers are two or one. Only on the surface are they two, deep inside they are one. Only in language will you appear two, the dancer and the witness, but deep down you are the one. The whole dancer is alert. Then only peace, equilibrium, silence will happen to you. If you are divided there will be tension, and that tension will not allow you to be totally here and now, to merge into existence.

So remember that: don't try to divide. Become the dancer, and still be aware. This happens. This I am saying through my experience. This I am saying through many others' experience who have been working with me. This will happen to you also. This may have happened to many already. But remember this: don't get split. Remain one and yet aware.

•••

3

ONLY KNOWING REMAINS

The first stage, to which contentment and bliss impart sweetness, springs from the innermost recesses of the seeker's heart, as if nectar has issued forth from the heart of the earth. At the inception of this stage the innermost recess becomes a field for the coming of the other stages.

Afterwards the seeker attains the second and third stages. Of the three, the third is the highest, because on its attainment all the modifications of ill come to an end. One who practices the three stages finds his ignorance dead, and on entering the fourth stage he sees everything, everywhere equally. At that moment he is so strongly embedded in the experience of non-duality—advaita—that the experience itself disappears. Thus, on attaining the fourth stage the seekers finds the world as illusory as a dream. So while the first three stages are called waking ones, the fourth is dreaming.

The first stage, to which contentment and bliss impart sweetness, springs from the innermost recesses of the seeker's heart, as if nectar has issued forth from the heart of the earth. At the inception of this stage the innermost recess becomes a field for the coming of the other stages. Afterwards the seeker attains the second ad third stages. Of the three, the third is the highest, because on its attainment all the modifications of will come to an end.

One who practices the three stages finds his ignorance dead, and on entering the fourth stage he sees everything, everywhere, equally. At that moment he is so strongly embedded in the experience of non-duality—*advaita*—that the experience itself disappears. Thus, an attaining the fourth stage the seeker finds the world as illusory s a dream. So while the first three stages are called waking ones, the fourth is dreaming.

THE FOURTH STAGE: The first is that of the oceanic feeling that Brahma exists everywhere—oneness. The one alone exists, the many are just its forms. They are not really divided, they only appear divided deep down they are one. The second stage is that of *vichar*– thought, contemplation and meditation–where mind has to be disciplined to become one-pointed. Because it can disappear only when it has become one-pointed, when the flux has stopped. That is, when you can remain with one thought as long as you wish. You have become the master then, and unless you are the master of the mind, the mind cannot disappear, it cannot cease to be; you cannot order it out of existence.

If you cannot order thoughts to stop, how can you order the whole mind to go out of existence? So in the second stage one has to drop thoughts by and by, and retain only one thought. When you have become capable of dropping thoughts, one day you can drop the mind itself, the whole thought-process. When thought-process is dropped, you cannot exist as an ego. You exist as consciousness, but not as mind; you are there, but not as an 'I'. We say 'I am'. When mind drops, the 'I' drops; you remain a pure 'amness.' Existence is there, rather, more abundant, more rich, more beautiful, but without the ego. There is no one who can say 'I', only 'amness' exists.

In the third stage, *vairagya*, non-attachment, you have to become alert-first of the objects of desire, the body, the world, and continuously practise and discipline yourself to become a witness. You are not the doer.

Your *karmas* may be the doers. God may be the doer, fate, or anything, but you are not the doer. You have to remain a witness, just a seer, an onlooker. And then this has also to be dropped. The idea that 'I am the witness', is also a sort of doing. Then non-attachment becomes complete, perfect. The third stage, this *Upanishad* says, is the highest of the three, now we will discuss the fourth.

The fourth is the state of advaita, non-duality. This word *'advaita'* has to be understood before we enter the *sutra*. This word is very meaningful. *Advaita* means literally non-duality, not two. They could have said one, but *Upanishads* never use the word 'one'. They say non-duality not two. And this is very significant, because if you say one, the two is implied, it becomes a positive statement. If you say there is only one, You are asserting something positive.

How can the one exist without the other? One cannot exist without the other. You cannot conceive of the figure one without other figures—two, three, four, fie. Many mathematicians have worked it out, particularly Leibniz in the West. He has tried to drop nine figures. Instead of nine he uses only two: one and two. In his calculations, three, four, six, seven, eight and nine are dropped, because he said it is just superstition to continue using ten figures. Why continue using ten figures?

You may not have observed: ten figures exist in mathematics not by any planning, but just because we have ten fingers. The primitives used to count on the fingers, so ten became the basic figure, and it has been taken all over the world. These ten figures, this basis of all arithmetic, was produced in India. That's why, even today, in all languages the words that denote these ten figures are basically Sanskrit: two is *dwi*, three is *tri*, fourth is *chaturth*, five is *panch*, six is *shashta*, seven is *sapta*, eight is *ashta*, nine is *nava*. These are basic roots.

These counting figures of ten, these ten digits, Leibniz says are useless. And science must try to work with the minimum, so he tried to minimize the digits. But he could not minimize more than two; he had to stop at two. So in Leibniz's system there is one, two, and then comes ten; three means ten, four means eleven, and so on, so forth. But he had to at least concede two, because just one cannot be conceived. You cannot use only one digit; ate least two are needed—the minimum requiremnt. The moment you say one, the two is implied, because one can exist only by the side of two. So *Upanishads*, never say that the Brahma is one, the truth is one. Rather, they use a negative term ; they say he is not two. So one is implied, but not directly asserted.

Secondly, about the total we cannot assert anything positive, we cannot say what it is. At the most we can say what it is not, we can negate. We cannot say directly, because once we say anything directly, it becomes defining, it becomes a limitation. If you say one, then you have limited; then a boundary has been drawn, then it cannot be infinite. When you simply say it is not two there is no boundary—the implication is infinite.

Upanishads say that the divine can be defined only by negatives, so they go on negating. They say, 'This is not Brahma, that is not Brahma.' And they never say directly, they never asset directly. You cannot point to the Brahma with a finger, because your finger will become a limitation. Then Brahma will be where your finger is pointing and nowhere else. You can point to the Brahma only with a closed fist, so you are not pointing anywhere; or—everywhere.

This negativity created many confusions, particularly in the West, because when for the first time the West came upon *Upanishads* in the last century and they were translated—first in German, then in English, and then French and other languages it was a very baffling thought. Because the Bible defines God positively; Jews, Christians, Mohammedans, define God very positively they say what he is. Hinduism defines God totally negatively—they say what he is not.

In the West this looked not very religious, because you cannot worship a negativity. You can worship only something positive, you can love only something positive, you can devote yourself to something positive. How can you devote yourself to something which is simply a denial, a negativity, a neti neti, neither this nor that? You cannot make an idol of a negative Brahma. How can you make an idol of a negative Brahma?

That's why Hindus conceived their highest conception of Brahma as Shivalinga. And people go on thinking that Shivalinga is just a phallic symbol. It is not just a phallic symbol; that is one of its implications. Shilvalinga is a symbol of zero, *shunya*, the negative. Shivalinga doesn't define any image; there is no image on it—no face, no eyes, nothing—just a zero, not even one. And the zero can be infinite. Zero has no boundaries: it begins nowhere, it ends nowhere.

How can you worship a zero? How can you pray to a zero? But Hindus have totally a different conception. They say prayer is not really an address to God, because you cannot address anything to him. Where will you address him? —he is nowhere or everywhere. So prayer is not really some address, rather, on the contrary, prayer is your inner mutation. Hindus say you cannot pray, but you can be in a prayerful mood. So prayer is not something you can do; prayer is something you can only be.

And prayer is not for God; prayer is for you. You pray, and through prayer you challenge. Nobody is listening to your prayer, and nobody is going to help you, nobody is going to follow your prayer, but just by praying your heart changes. Through prayer, if authentic, you become different—your assertion changes you.

In the south there is one old temple. If you go in the temple there is no deity; the place for the deity is vacant, empty. If you ask the priest, ' where is the deity? Whom to worship? And this is a temple—to whom does this temple belong? Who is the deity of this temple? The priest will tell you, 'this is the tradition of this temple—that we don't have any deity. The whole temple is the deity. You cannot look for the deity in a particular direction. He is everywhere—that's why the place is vacant.

The whole universe is Brahma. And this is such a vast phenomenon that positive terms will only make it finite, hence negativity—it is one of the highest conceptions possible. And this negativity reached its most logical extreme in Buddha, because he would not even negate. Because he said, ' Even if you negate, indirectly you assert, and every assertion is blasphemy.

Jews could have understood this. They have no name for God. Yahweh is not a name, it is just a symbol. Or, it means 'the nameless'. And in the old Jewish old world before Jesus, the name was not to be asserted by everybody. Only the chief priest in the temple of Solomon, once a year was allowed to assert the name. So once a year all the Jews would gather together at the great temple of Solomon, and the highest priest would asset the name 'Yahweh.' And it is not a name; the very word means 'the nameless.'

Nobody was allowed to assert the name, because how can the finite assert the infinite? And whatsoever you say will be wrong because you are wrong. Whatsoever you say belongs to you, it comes through you, you are present in it. So unless you had become so empty that you were no more, you wee not allowed to assert the name. The highest priest was the man who had become just an emptiness. And to assert the name, for the whole year he would remain silent. He would prepare, he would become totally empty, no thought was allowed in the mind. For one year he would wait, prepare, become empty, become a nonentity, a nobody. When the right moment came he would stand just like an emptiness. The man was not there; there was nobody. The mind was not there. And then he would asset 'Yahweh.'

This tradition stopped, because it became more and more difficult to find persons who could become non-entities, who could become nothingness, who could become anatta, non-being, who could destroy themselves so completely that God could assert through them, who could become just like a passage, just like a flute, empty, so that God could sing through it.

Buddha went to the very extreme. If you asked him about God, he would remain totally silent. Once it happened, Ananda, his chief disciple, was sitting with Buddha, and a man came, a very cultured, refined philosopher, a great Brahmin. And he asked, ' Bhante, tell me something about the ultimate.'

Buddha looked at him, remained silent, then closed his eyes. Ananda became disturbed, because this man was very useful. This Brahmin had a great following, thousands followed him; if he was converted, then thousands would become Buddhist. And Buddha remained silent; he didn't answer him. The man, the Brahmin, bowed down, thanked Buddha and went away.

The moment he left, Ananda asked, 'What are you doing? You have missed a great opportunity. This man is no ordinary man. Thousands follow him, he is great scholar. Thousands worship him; his word is significant. If he becomes a Buddhist, if he follows you, many will follow automatically. And you didn't answer him!'

Buddha said, 'For a good horse even the shadow of a whip is enough. The shadow of the whip is enough; you need not beat him. He is converted.'

Ananda was not convinced, but next day he saw the man coming with all his followers, his disciples; thousands followed, great scholars. He had a big ashram and they all were coming. Ananda couldn't believe his eyes. What was happening? And Buddha had not answered the man.

So again in the night he asked, what was happened? You have done a miracle. I was there. You remained completely silent; not only silent, you closed your eyes. And I thought this was insulting. The man had come with so much enquiry and you were rejecting him.'

Buddha said, 'This is the subtlest answer. He knows that nothing can be said about the ultimate. Had I said anything the man would have gone, because the very saying would have shown that my ultimate is not ultimate—it could be defined, something could be said about it. Nothing can be said. And that's why I even closed my eyes because, who knows, he may have thought that I was saying something through my eyes. So I completely became silent, closed my eyes—this was my answer. And for a good horse even the shadow of the whip is enough. You need not beat him.'

Upanishads are negative about the Brahma. That's why they say, 'the non-dual', that which is not two. Now we will enter the *sutra*:

The first stage, to which contentment and bliss impart sweetness, springs from the innermost recesses of the seeker's heart.

As I said to you, the first is the feeling, the first is the heart. The first stage belongs to the heart, and only the heart can know contentment and bliss. If you are in contact with your heart, you will know contentment and bliss, just like sweet springs flowing towards you, filling you, over-flooding you. But we don't have the contact with the heart. The heart is beating, but we don't have the contact.

You will have to understand it, because just by having a heart, don't go on thinking that you are in contact with it. You are not in contact with many things in your body; you are just carrying your body. Contact means a deep sensitivity. You may not even feel your body. It happens that only when you are ill, do you feel your body. There is a headache; then you feel the head. Without the headache there is no contact with the head. There is pain in the leg; you become aware of the leg. You become aware only when something goes wrong.

If everything is okay you remain completely unaware, and really, that is the moment when contact can be made—when everything is okay. Because when something goes wrong, then that contact is made with illness, with something that has gone wrong, and the well being is no more there. You have the head right now; then headache comes and you make the contact. The contact is made not with the head but with the headache. With the head, contact is possible only when there is no headache, and the head is filled with a well-being. But we have almost lost the capacity. We don't have any contact when we are okay. So our contact is just an emergency measure. There is a headache: some repair is needed, some medicine is needed something ahs to be done, so you make the contact and do something.

Try to make contact with your body when everything is good. Just lie down on the grass, close the eyes, and feel the sensation that is going on within, the well being that is bubbling. Lie down in a river. The water is touching the body, and every cell is being cooled. Feel inside how that coolness enters cell by cell, goes deep into the body. Body is a great phenomenon; one of the miracles of nature.

Sit in the sun. Let the sun-rays penetrate the body. Feel the warmth as it moves within, as it goes deeper, as it touches your blood-cells, and reaches to the very bones. And sun is life, the very source. So with closed eyes just feel what is happening. Remain alert, watch and enjoy. By and by you will become aware of a very subtle harmony, a very beautiful music continuously going on inside. Then you have the contact with the body. Otherwise you carry a dead body.

It is just like this: a person who loves his car has a different type of contact and relationship with the car than a person who doesn't. A person who doesn't love his car goes on driving it, and he treats it as a mechanism. But a person who loves his car will become aware of even the smallest change in the mood of the car, the finest change of sound. Something is changing in the car and suddenly he will become aware of it. No one else has heard it. The passengers are sitting there, they have not heard it. But a slight change in the sound of the engine, any clicking, any change, and the person who loves his car will become aware of it.

He has a deep contact. He is not only driving, the car is not just a mechanism. Rather, he has spread himself into the car and he has allowed the car to enter him. Your body can be used as a mechanism; then you need not be very sensitive about it. And the body goes on saying many things you never hear, because you don't have any contact.

In Soviet Russian a new research has been going on for thirty years. Now they have concluded many things. One result which is very revealing is this: that whenever a disease happens, before it happens, for six months continuously the body goes on giving signals to you. Six months is too long a time! A disease is going to happen in 1975. In the middle of 1974 the body will start giving you signals, but you don't hear, you don't understand, you don't know. When the disease has happened already, only then will you become aware. Or even then you may not be aware. Your doctor first becomes aware that you have some deep trouble inside.

The person who has been doing this research for thirty years has now made films and cameras which can detect a disease before it actually happens.

He says that the disease can be treated, and the patient will never become aware of whether it existed or not. If a cancer is going to happen next year, it can be treated right now. There are no physical indications, but just in the body-electricity things are changing—not in the body, in the body-electricity, in the bio-energy, things are changing. First they will change in the bio-energy, and then they will descend to the physical.

If they can be treated in the bio-energy layer then they will never come to the physical body. Because of this research it will become possible in the coming century that no one need be ill; there will be no more need to go to the hospital. Before the disease actually comes to the body it can be treated, but it has to be detected by a mechanical device. You cannot detect it, and you are there, living in the body. There is no contact.

You may have heard many stories that Hindu sannyasins, rishis, Zen monks, Buddhist bhikkus, declare their death before it happens. And you may be surprised to know that the declaration is always made six months before it happen—never more before, always six months before. Many saints have declared that they are going to die, but just six months before. It is not accidental; those six months are meaningful. Before the physical body dies, the bio-energy starts dying, and a person who is in deep contact with his bi-energy knows that now the energy has started shrinking. Life means spreading, death means shrinking. He feels that the life-energy is shrinking; he declares that he will be dead within six months. Zen monks are known to have even chosen how to die, because they know.

It happened once, one Zen monk was to die, so he asked his disciples, 'Suggest to me how to die. In what posture.'

That man was a little eccentric, a little crazy, a mad old man, but very beautiful. His disciples started laughing; they thought that he may have been joking because he was always joking. So somebody suggested, 'How about dying standing in the corner of the temple?

The man said, 'But I have heard a story that in the past one monk has died standing, so that won't be good. Suggest something unique.'

So somebody said, 'While just walking in the garden, die.'

He said, 'I have heard that somebody in China once died walking.'

Then someone suggested a really unique idea. 'Stand in *sirshasan*, headstand, and die.

Nobody has ever died standing on the head; it is very difficult to die standing on the head. Even to sleep standing on the head is impossible; death is too difficult. Even to sleep is impossible and death is a great sleep. It is impossible—even ordinary sleep is impossible.

The man accepted the idea. He enjoyed it. He said, 'This is good,

They thought that he was just joking, but he stood in *sirshasan*. They became afraid—what is he doing? And what to do now? And they thought he was almost dead. It was weird—a dead person standing in *sirshasan*. They became scared, so somebody suggested, 'He has a sister in the near by monastery who is a great nun. Go and fetch her. She is elder sister of this man and may do something with him. She knows him well.'

The sister came. It is said that she came and said, 'Ikkyu' (Ikkyu was the name of the monk) don't be foolish! This is no way to die.

Ikkyu laughed, jumped from his *sirshasan*, and said, 'Okay so what is right way?'

She said, 'Sit in *padmasan*, Buddha posture, and die. This is no way to die. And you have always been a foolish man, everybody will laugh.'

So it is said he sat in *padmasan* and died, and the sister let. A beautiful man. But how could he decide that he was going to die? And even to choose the posture! The bio-energy started shrinking; he could feel it—but this feeling comes only when you have a deep contact, not only with the surface of the body, but with the roots.

So first try to be more and more sensitive about your body. Listen to it; it goes on saying many things, and you are so head-oriented you never listen to it. Whenever there is a conflict between your mind and body, body is almost always going to be right more than your mind, because body is natural, your mind is societal, body belongs to this vast nature and your mind belongs to your society, your particular society, age, time; body has deep roots in existence; mind is just wavering on the surface. But you always listen to the mind, you never listen to the body. Because of this long habit, contact is lost.

You have the heart, and heart is the root, but you don't have any contact. First start having contact with the body. Soon you will become aware that the whole body vibrates around the center of the heart, just as the whole solar system moves around the sun. Hindus have called the heart the sun of the body. The whole body is a solar system, and moves around the heart. You became alive when the heart started beating; you will die when the heart stops beating. The heart remains the solar center of your body—become alert to it. But you can become alert, by and by, only if you become alert to the whole body.

While hungry, why not meditate a little? There is no hurry. While hungry just close your eyes and meditate on the hunger, on how the body is feeling. You may have lost contact, because our hunger is less bodily, more mental. You eat everyday at one o'clock. You look at the watch; it is one—so then you feel hunger. And the clock may not be right. If somebody says, 'That clock has stopped at midnight. It is not functioning. It is only eleven o'clock, the hunger disappears. This hunger is false,this hungar is just habitual, because the mind creates it, it not the body. Mind says, 'One o'clock: you are hungry.' You have to be hungry. You have always been hungry at one o'clock, so you are hungry.

Our hunger is almost ninety-nine percent habitual. Go on a fast for a few days to feel real hunger, and you will be surprised. For the first three or four days you will feel very hungry. On the fourth or fifth day you will not feel so hungry. This is illogical, because as the fast grows, you should feel more and more hungry. But after the third day you will feel less hungry, and after the seventh day you may completely forget hunger. After the eleventh day almost everybody forgets hunger completely and the body feels absolutely okay. Why? And if you continue the fast….Those who have done much work on fasting say that only after the twenty-first day will real hunger happen again.

So it means that for three days your mind was insisting that you were hungry because you had not taken food, but it was not hunger. Within three days the mind gets fed up with telling you; you are not listening, you are so indifferent. On the fourth day the mind doesn't say anything;

the body doesn't feel hunger. For three weeks you will not feel hunger, because you have accumulated so much fat—that fat will do. You will feel hunger only after the third week. And this is for normal bodies.

If you have too much fat accumulated, you may not feel hungry even after the third week. And there is a possibility to accumulate enough fat to live on for three months, ninety days. When the body is finished with the accumulated fat, then for the first time real hunger will be felt. But it will be difficult. You can try with thirst; that will be easy. For one day don't take water, and wait. Don't drink out of habit. Just wait and see what thirst means: what thirst would mean if you were in a desert.

Lawrence of Arabia has written in his memoirs, 'For the first time in my life, when I was once lost in the desert, I became aware of what thirst is. Because before that there was no need. Whenever my mind said, "Now you are thirsty," I took water. In the desert, lost, no water with me, and no way to find an oasis, for the first time I became thirsty. And that thirst was something wonderful—the whole of the body, every cell, asking for water. It became a phenomenon.' If you take water in that type thirst, it will give you a contentment that you cannot know just by drinking through habit.

So I say to you that Mahavir, and persons like Mahavir, have known the real taste of food. You cannot know it. Because for three months

Mahavir would fast, then he would go begging. And he would go begging only when the body would say, not the mind. When the body would say, 'Now I am exhausted completely,' and the hunger gripped the whole body and every cell of it asked, then he would go begging. He would not listen to the mind. He must have tasted food as no one has ever tasted on this earth. But Jains think completely differently: they think that he was tasteless, they think that he had no taste. My feeling is, only he knew what taste is, and he knew it with his whole body, his whole being.

You know only by your tongue, and that tongue is very deceptive. That tongue has been serving the mind so long it is no more serving the body. The tongue can deceive you; it has become a slave of the mind. It can go on saying, 'Go on eating. It is very beautiful.' It is not serving the body anymore. Otherwise the tongue would say, 'stop!' The tongue would say, 'Whatsoever you are eating is useless. Don't eat!' Even the tongues of cows and buffalos are more body rooted than your tongue. You cannot force a buffalo to eat any type of grass—she chooses. You cannot force your dog to eat when he is ill—he will immediately go out, eat some grass, and vomit. He is more in contact with his body.

First one has to become deeply aware of this phenomenon of the body. A revival of the body, a resurrection, is needed—you are carrying a dead body. Then only will you feel, by and by, that the whole body with all its desires, thirsts and hungers is revolving around the heart. Then the beating heart is not only a mechanism, it is the beating life, it is the very pulsation of life. That pulsation gives contentment and bliss.

Contentment and bliss impart sweetness.

Your, whole being becomes sweet, a sweetness surrounds you, it becomes your aura. Whenever a person is in contact with his heart, you will immediately fall in love with him. Immediately, the moment you see him, you will fall in love with him. You don't know why. He has a sweetness around him. That sweetness your mind may not be able to detect, but you heart detects it immediately.

He has an aura. The moment you come in his aura, you are intoxicated. You feel a longing for him, you feel an attraction, a magnetic force working. You may not be consciously aware of what is happening; you may simply say, 'I don't know why I am attracted,' but this is the reason. A person who lives in his heart has a milieu around him of sweetness—sweetness flows around him. You are flooded with it whenever you are in contact with that person.

Buddha, Jesus, attracted millions of persons, and the reason is that thy lived in the heart. Otherwise it was impossible. What Buddha demanded was impossible to do. Thousands of people left their homes, became beggars with him, moved with him in all types of sufferings, austerities and enjoyed it. This is a miracle. And those who left their homes were rich, affluent people, because India knew the golden age in the time of Buddha. It was at its highest peak of richness. Just as America is today, India was at that moment. At that moment the West was just wild; no civilization existed really. The West was totally uncivilized at the time of Buddha, and India was at its golden peak.

Buddha attracted millions of people who were rich, living in comfort, and they moved and became beggars. What filled them, what attracted them, what was the cause? Even they couldn't explain what the cause was. This is the cause: Whenever a person of heart is there, a person who lives in his heart, he imparts around him vibrations of sweetness. Just being in his presence, being near him, you feel a sudden joy for no visible cause. He is not giving you anything, he is not giving you any physical comfort. On the contrary, he may lead you into physical uncomfort; through him, you may have to pass many sufferings—but you will enjoy those sufferings.

Buddha was dying, and Ananda, his disciple, was weeping. So Buddha said, 'Why are you weeping?'

Ananda said, 'With you I can, move on this earth; millions of times I can be reborn, and it will not be suffering. I can suffer everything. Just if you are there, then this sansar, which you call dukkha, suffering, is no more suffering. But without you, even nirvana will not be blissful.'

Such a sweetness surrounded Buddha, such a sweetness surrounded St. Francis, such a sweetness surround all those who have lived through the heart. Their charisma is that they live in their heart.

Jesus was not a very learned man. He was just a villager, he remained a carpenter's son. He was talking in people's ways, ordinary parables. If someone gives you Jesus' parables, his statements, without saying that these belong to Jesus, you will throw the book, you will never read it again. But he influenced people, impressed so much, that Christianity became the greatest religion of the world. Half the earth belongs now to Christianity, to a carpenter's son who was not educated, not cultured. What is this mystery? How did it happen? He was not a man of knowledge, he was not like Bertrand Russell.. Bertrand Russell could have easily defeated him in any argument. It is not difficult to conceive of that, Jesus could be defeated easily.

It has happened in India in just the last century. Ramakrishna, Vivekananda's master, was here. He was a man of heart, completely uneducated, not in anyway proficient in the scriptures. He has no logic, no arguing force, could not convince anybody. It happened that one of the greatest scholars ever born in India, Keshavchandra Sen, went to see Ramakrishna. He was a great scholar, very logical, rational, argumentative, so many people followed just to see what would happen. because everybody knew, it was decided, that Ramakrishna would be defeated immediately. Nobody could argue with Keshavchandra.

Ramakrishna's disciples were very sacred. They also knew that this Keshavchandra was going to be difficult, and once Keshavchandra defeated Ramakrishna—and he could defeat him on any point, there was no question about it—then that defeat would spread all over the country. So what to do? How to protect Ramakrishna? They started thinking. They were so worried they couldn't sleep for days. Whenever they said anything to Ramakrishna he laughed and he said, 'Let him come. I am waiting.'

Then that day came; the whole *ashram* was sad. Keshavchandra came, very proud, very egoistic; And he had reason to be proud and egoistic, he was one of the finest intellects, a genius. And many of his followers came; professors of the universities, pundits, scholars, men who knew the Vedas—there was a big, big crowd of many renowned persons. Keshavchandra started the argument 'Does God exist?'

So ramakrishna said, 'you say whatsoever you want to say.'

Keshavchndra started critcizing, saying that there is no God, but by and by he became very uncomfortable, because whenever he would give an argument against God, Ramakrishna would laugh and enjoy so much that there was no argument. And he would say, 'Right! Absolutely right!' He was not confuting, he was not going against, so the whole thing became nonsense, because you can defeat a person only when he argues. The very effort to win was futile because there was no one to defeat. Then by and by he became sad, and the whole thing looked useless. Then he asked, 'Ramakrishna, why do you go on saying 'yes'? I am saying God is no more!' Keshavhandra thought, ' He is so foolish, he cannot understand what I am saying.'

Ramakrishna said only one thing: ' I was never so convinced that God is before, I saw you, But the moment I saw you, I was absolutely convinced that God is.'

Keshavchandra asked, 'Why?'

Ramakrishan said, ' How could such a beautiful mind exist without God? Such a refined intellect. You convince me that God is! I am a poor man, uneducated; such a mind like me can exist even without God, but such a mind like you? - Impossible!'

Keshavchandra had to touch his feet, and say, ' You have defeated!' He became a life-long devotee to Ramakrishna. What was the miracle? What was the charisma?— a person living in the heart. Keshavchandra is reported to have said to his followers, 'This man is dangerous, don't go near him. He has converted me, not saying anything, just being present there, laughing, enjoying. And he filled me with such sweetness I have never known. Just in his presence I have felt the first ecstasy of my life, the peak experience. The unknown has touched me.

The first stage, to which contentment and bliss impart sweetness, springs from the innermost recess of the seeker's heart, as if nectar has issued forth from the heart of the earth. At the inception of this stage the innermost recess becomes a field for the coming of the other stages. Afterwards the seeker attains the second and third stages. Of the three, the third is the highest, because on its attainment all the modifications of will come to an end.

All the modifications of will come to an end. The third is the highest. And the reason? Let it penetrate deep in your heart. The third is the highest. Why?—because all the modifications of will come to an end.

Your will is the cause of your ego. You think you can do something, you think you will do something. You think you have got will-power, you think that there is a possibility for you to struggle with existence and win. Will means the attitude to fight, the attitude to conquer, the attitude to struggle. Will is the force of violence in you.

Bertrand Russell has written a book: 'Conquest of Nature' This is impossible to conceive in the East. Lao Tzu cannot use these words, 'conquest of nature', because who will conquer nature? You are nature. Who will conquer nature? You are not separate from it. But the West has lived for these twenty centuries with this wrong concept—the conquest of nature. We have to defeat nature, to destroy it, to cripple it, to force it to follow is. You cannot win, this whole struggle is nonsense, because you are nature. The is no division. The East says, 'Follow nature, become nature. Leave the will. The will is the cause of misery. The will is the door to hell.'

The third is thought to be highest, because when you leave all desires there is no need for the will—because will is need to fulfill desires. You have desires; you need will. There are many books in the West and particularly in America, which go on teaching will-power. And they are sold in millions, they are best sellers, because everybody thinks that he has to conquer and create will-power. People even come to me, to such a person who is absolutely against will, and they say, ' Help us. How can we have more will-power?'

Will is your impotence. Because of will you are defeated, because you are doing something absolutely absurd, something which cannot happen. When you leave will, only then will you be powerful. When there is no will you have become impotent. Omnipotent also you can become when there is no will, because then you are one with the universe; then the whole universe is your power.

With the will you are a fragment fighting with the whole existence, with such a small quantity of energy. And that energy is also given by the universe. Universe is so playful that it even allows you to fight with it, it gives you the energy. Universe gives you the breath, universe gives you the life, and enjoys your fighting. It is just as a father enjoys fighting with child, and challenges the child to fight. The child starts fighting, and the father falls down and helps the child to win. This is a game for the father. The child may be serious, may get mad; he will think, ' I have conquered.'

In the West this childishness has become the source of many miseries: Hiroshima, Nagasaki, these two world wars, are because of this will. Science should not be any more the conquest of nature. Science must now become the way towards nature—surrender to nature, not conquest to nature. And unless science becomes Taoist—surrender to nature—science is going to eliminate the whole of humanity from this earth. This planet will be destroyed by science. And science can destroy only because science has become associated with this absurd notion of conquest.

Man has a will-power. Every will is against nature; your will is against nature. When you can say totally, 'Not mine, but your will should be done'—'your' means the divine, the totality, the wholeness—for the first time you become powerful. But this power doesn't belong to you; you are just a passage. The power belongs to the cosmos.

The third is the highest, because all the modifications of will come to an end. Not only the will, but the modification—because will can get modified. We saw that the Upanishad divides desirelessness, non-attachment, in two parts. First: when you make effort to be non-attach—that too is a modification of the will. You struggle, your control, you detach yourself, you make all the efforts to remain a witness. Those efforts to remain a witness belong to your will, so really that is not real non-attachment, just a rehearsal; not real, just a training ground.

Non-attachment will become real only in the second stage, when even this struggle to be a witness has dropped; when even the idea that 'I am a witness' has dropped; when there is no more conflict between you and existence. No more, no more any conflict, you simply flow with it.

Lao Tzu reported to have said, 'I struggled hard, but I was defeated again and again, fortunately.' He says, 'Fortunately, I was defeated again and again. No effort succeeded, and then I realized—against who am I fighting? Again myself I am fighting; against the greater part of my own being, I am fighting. It is as if my hand is fighting against my body, and the hand belongs to the body . It can fight, but the hand has the energy through the body.' Lap Tzu says, 'When I realized that I am part of this cosmos, that I am not separate—the cosmos breathes in me, lives in me, and I am fighting it—then the fight dropped. Then I became like a deaf leaf.

Why like a dead leaf? Because the dead leaf has no will of her own. The wind comes, takes the dead leaf; the dead leaf goes with the wind. The wind is going north. The dead leaf dosen't say, 'I want to go to the south. The dead leaf goes to the north. Then the wind changes its course, starts flowing towards the south. The deaf leaf doesn't say, you are contradictory. first you were going to the north, now you are going to south. Now I want to go to the north.'

No, that leaf doesn't say anything. She moves to south, she moves to north, and if the wind stops she falls down on the ground and rests. She doesn't say, 'This was not the right time for me to rest.' When the wind raises her into the sky the dead leaf doesn't say, 'I am the peak of existence.'

When she falls to the ground she is not frustrated. A dead leaf simply has no will of her own. 'Thy will be done.' She moves with the wind, wheresoever it leads. She has got no goal, she has no purpose of her own.

Lao Tzu says, 'When I became like a dead leaf, then everything was achieved. Then there was nothing to be achieved any more. Then all bliss became mine.'

All the modifications of will come to an end.

One who practices the three stages finds his ignorance dead, and on entering the fourth stage he sees everything, everywhere, equally.

Two things: One who practices these three stages finds his ignorance dead. Your ignorance cannot become dead by accumulating knowledge. You can accumulate all the knowledge available in the world; you can become an 'Encyclopedia Britannica', but that won't help. You can become a walking encyclopedia, but your ignorance will not be dead through that. Rather, on the contrary, your ignorance will become hidden, secret;

it will move to the deep recesses of the heart. So on the surface you will be knowledgeable, and deep down you will remain ignorant. This is what has happened, and all the universities go on helping this.

Your ignorance is never dead; it is alive, working. And just on the surface you are decorated; you are painted being. Your knowledge is painted just on the surface and deep down you remain ignorant. The knowledge, real knowledge, can happen only when the ignorance is dead. Before that, knowledge will remain information—borrowed, not yours, not authentic—it has not happened to you. It is not a lived experience, but only words, verbal, scriptural.

And ignorance can become dead only when you practice these first three stages, because ignorance is a mode of life, not a question of information. It is a way of life, a wrong way of life, that creates ignorance. It is not just a question of memory, of how much you know, or how much you don't know—that is not the point. That's why Ramakrishna can become wise and Keshavchandra remains ignorant. Jesus became enlightened, and Pontius Pilate remained ignorant. He was more cultured than Jesus, more educated; he had all the education that was possible. He was the governor general, the viceroy; he knew whatsoever could be known through books. And in the last moment before Jesus was sent to the cross, he asked him a very philosophical question.

Nietzsche wrote about Pontius Pilate, because Nietzsche was always against Jesus. When he became mad in the end–and he was bound to become mad because his whole way of life, the whole style was madness— he started signing his signature as 'Anti-Christ, Friedrich Nietzsche.' He would never sign his signature without writing before it, Anti-Christ.' He was absolutely against Jesus. He says that only Pontius Pilate was the man who knew, and Jesus was simply an ignorant carpenter's son. And the reason that he proposes is that in the last moment before Jesus went to the cross, Pontius Pilate asked him, 'What is truth?' This is one the most significant philosophical questions which has always been asked, and philosophers enjoy answering it—but nobody has answered yet. To Nietzsche , Jesus looks foolish. He writes that when Pontius Pilate asked Jesus 'What is truth?' he was asking precisely the peak question, the sole question, the ultimate question, the base of all philosophy, the base of all enquiry—and Jesus remained silent.

Nietzsche says that was because in the first place Jesus would not have understood what Pontius Pilate meant, and secondly, he could not answer because he didn't know what truth is. He was ignorant, that's why he remained silent. And I say to you, he remained silent because he knew, and he knew well that this question can never be answered verbally.

Pontius Pilate was foolish; educated, well educated, but foolish—because this question cannot be asked in such a way, and it cannot be answered when a person is going to be hanged. For the answer to this question, Pontius Pilate would have had to live with Jesus for years, because the whole life has to be transformed, only then can the answer be given. Or, the transformed life itself becomes the answer, there is no need to give it.

Jesus remained silent; that shows he was a wise man. Had he given any answer, to me he would have proved that he was ignorant. Even Jesus' followers became a little uncomfortable, because they thought that had he answered Pontius Pilate, and had Pilate been convinced that his answer was true, there would have been no crucifixion. But crucifixion is better than answering a foolish question with a foolish answer. Crucifixion is always better than that. And Jesus chose crucifixion rather than answering this foolish question. Because such questions need a mutation in life; you have to work upon yourself.

Truth is not something which can be handed over to you. You will have to raise your consciousness; you will have to come to the climax of your being. Only from there, the glimpses becomes possible. And when you die completely to your ego, truth is revealed, never before. It is not a philosophical enquiry, it is a religious transformation.

One who practices the three stages finds his ignorance dead, and on entering the fourth stage he sees everything, everywhere, equally. At that moment he is so strongly embedded in the experince of non-duality-*advaita*—that the experience itself disappears.

This is very subtle and delicate point. Let it go deep in your heart. He is so embedded in the fourth stage… After the three stages the fourth follows automatically. The three have to be practised, the three have to be deeply rooted in your being through your effort—the fourth happens. Suddenly you become aware that there is non-duality, only one exists—one being, one existence.

He is so strongly embedded in the experience of *advaita*—non-duality—that the experience itself disappears.

Because for experience to exist, duality is needed. So *Upanishads* say you cannot experience God. If you experience God, then the God remains separate and you remain separate, because only the other can be experienced. Experience divides. This is the deepest message of all the Upanishads: experience divides. Because whenever you say experience, it means there are three things: the experiencer, the experienced, and the relationship between the two, the experience.

Upanishads say the God cannot be known, because knowledge divides the knower, the known and the knowledge. If really you have become one, how can you experience? So even the experience disappears. Upanishads say a person who claims he has experienced the divine is false; his claim proves that he is false. A knower cannot claim, one who has really experienced the divine cannot claim, because the very experience disappears. Buddha says again and again, 'Don't ask me what I have experienced. If I say anthing then I am not true. Rather come near me, and you also go through the experience.'

One man came, one Maulangputta, and he asked Buddha serious questions. Buddha said, 'You wait for one year, and then I will give you the answers. And for one year you have to follow me, whatsoever I say, with no argument, no discussion. You put your reason aside. For one year be with me and experience, and after one year has elapsed you can ask all your questions, bring all your reason back, and then I will answer you.'

While Buddha was saying this and Maulangputta was being convinced, one *sannyasin*, one bhikku of Buddha, Sariputta, who was siting under a tree, started laughing. Maulangputta became uncomfortable. He asked Sariputta, why are you laughing? What is wrong?

Sariputta said, 'Don't be deceived. This man is a deceiver. He deceived me the same way. How I cannot ask, so he need not answer. If you want to ask at all, ask now. After one year it will be too late.'

Then one year passed, and Maulangputta waited, meditated, became more and more silent, and started realizing why Sariputta was laughing—because the questions were disappearing. One year passed and then he started hiding, because if he met Buddha, he would say, 'Now, where are the questions?'

But Buddha remembered. Exactly on the day when he had come one year before, exactly on that day as he was hiding behind ten thousands monks, Buddha said, ' Where is Maulangputta ? He must come now, the time has come. Bring your reason and bring all your questions. I am prepared to answer.'

Maulangputta stood, and said, 'You are really a deceiver. That Sariputta was right—because now I have got no questions!'

Buddha says, 'Experience –and you cannot even claim that you have experienced.' But who will experience?—three is no other. Who will experience whom?—even the experience itself disappears. There is nothing like God experience; it is only in the minds of the ignorant. The knowers know that God disappears and the 'I' disappears, the duality disappears. Knowing is there, but the knower is not and the known is not.

Because of this Mahavir has used a beautiful word. He calls it *Kaivalya gyan*; he calls it, 'only knowing remains'—only knowing, neither the known nor the knower. You disappear; the God you were seeking disappears, because really the God you were seeking was created by you. It was your ignorance that was seeking. Your God was part of your ignorance. It is bound to be. How can you seek the real God? You don't know it.

You project your God through your ignorance; you seek it. All your heavens are part of your ignorance. All your truths are part of your ignorance. You seek them. And then your ignorance disappears. When your ignorance disappears where will those Gods remain who were created by your ignorance? They will also disappear.

It happened, when Rinzai became enlightened he asked for a cup of tea. His disciples said, 'This seems to be profane.'

And he said, 'The whole thing was foolishness: the seeking, the seeker, the sought. The whole thing was foolishness. You just give me a cup of tea! None existed. The seeker was false, the sought was false, so of course, the seeking was false. It was a cosmic joke.'

That's why I say there is no purpose—God is joking with you. The The moment you can understand the joke, you are enlightened. Then the whole thing becomes a play; even the experience disappears.

Thus, an attaining the fourth stage the seeker finds the world as illusory as a dream So while the first three stages are called waking ones, the fourth is dreaming.

When the fourth stage is attained, when even God disappears, when the God-seeker, the worshipper disappears, this whole world becomes like a dream, Not that it is not there. It is there, but like a dream; it has no substantiality in it. It is a mental phenomenon, it is a thought process. You enjoy it, you live in it—but you know that this is all a dream .

This is the Hindu concept of the world: they say it is a dream in the mind of God. It is just as you dream in the night: when you dream you can create a reality in the dream, and you never suspect that this is a dream and you are the creator. The beauty is this—that you are the creator, you are the projector, and you cannot suspect that it is a just dream. Hindus say that as there are private dreams, individual dreams, this is the collective dream—God dreaming the world. You are a dream object in the God's dream. We take dreams to be real, and Hindus say the reality is a dream. I will tell you one anecdote.

Once it happened Mulla Nasrudin was fast asleep with his wife in the bed. The wife started dreaming; she has a very beautiful dream.

One charming young man was making lover to her, and she was enjoying it. very much. She was old, ugly and he was a very charming young prince and she was enjoying Suddenly in the dream, when she was enjoying the love making,. Mulla Nasrudin entered from the roof-in the dream. She became afraid. She became so afraid and disturbed that she said loudly, very much. She was old, ugly and he was a very charming young prince and she was enjoying: Suddenly in the dream, when she was enjoying the love making, Mulla Nasrudin entered from the roof-in the dream. She became afraid. She became so afraid and disturbed that she said loudly, ' My God, my husband! She said it so loudly that Mulla heard it and jumped out of the window. He thought he was sleeping with some other woman.

Our dream are realities for us. For *Upanishads*, our reality is just a dream.

●●●

4

WHEN THE COIN DISAPPEARS

Some mystics have been very introverted and silent. In your own case, you appear to be moving both introvertedly and extrovertedly without any difficulty. Please explain how this is possible.

The mind goes on dividing on every level of being. Wherever the mind looks, immediately it divides; division, to divide, is the nature of the mind. So we say, 'above and below'; we say 'up and down'; we say 'this world and the other world'; we say 'life and death;' we say in and out'; 'extroversion and introversion—but all thee division are of the mind. The below is part of the above, the beginning of the above; up is nothing but the extension of down. Life and death are not two, but the same energy arising is life, the same energy dissolving is death. Out and in are not two; the division is only mental.

But we exist extrovertedly; we exist outside. The ordinary man exist outside; he never goes in. He moves further and further out, because desires can be fulfilled only in the outside; some object is needed to fulfill them. The object can be found in the outside; there is no object within—there is only subjectivity, there is only you. You need something to fulfill desires, so you move in the world. The out is created because desiresd are moving outwardly.

Then a moment comes in everyone's life when you get frustrated with this whole business—desires, the search for them ,the objects—and you come to realize that the whole thing is futile. Then the other extreme arises in the mind: 'Don't go out, go in!' Then you simply reverse the whole process. Before you were going out, now you start going in, before you were for the out, now you have become against it.

This type of mind which has become against the world, the out, is just the same man, the same mind, standing on its head. You are standing on your feet, he is standing on his head, but he is the same man, there is no difference. The difference comes into being only when you are not moving at all, neither out nor in; when the division between out and in has dropped.

And this can drop only when you are not. If you are, then you are bound to divide the within and the without. When the ego disappears, which is within? Where is within then? It was around your ego. If ego has disappeared, then where is within and where is without? They were in relation to your ego. When the ego has disappeared, out and in disappear—

then there is no introversion and extroversion. Man exists as extrovert or introvert, but when you transcend the ego you have transcended the man. Then you simply exist—the within and without have become one, the boundaries have disappeared.

Just as we are sitting inside this room. If these walls disappear, then what will be the inside and what will be the outside? Then the inside will become the outside, and the outside will become the inside. In actuality, even now this very moment, is the space outside and the space within really divided? can you divide it? You can create walls, but you cannot divide it, you cannot cut space. And you can use the inside only because of the doors. Otherwise you cannot use the inside. And from the door it same: from the door the inside and the outside are one.

Lao Tzu uses this symbol very much. He goes on saying that the room is valuable not because of the walls, but because of the doors. The room has value not because of the walls, but because of the doors--and doors mean no division between outside and inside. Doors are the link: you can come in and you can go out. But if you destroy the walls, then the division disappears. When the ego drops, the division disappears.

So Jung's psychology will be meaningless when the ego has disappeared. Jung divides mind into two: the extrovert mind and the introvert mind—but this is a division of the mind, not of consciousness. Consciousness is just like the space; mind is just the walls. But you can use mind only because mind has few doors, and through those doors the within moves in the without, and the without goes on moving into the within.

A mystic is a person whose mind has disappeared: he has attained to no-mind. So if a mystic insists that I am against the world, he is not a mystic really; he still belongs to the world, because he still carries the same division.

I will tell you an anecdote. It happened once two Zen monks were returning to their monastery. The evening was just near, the sun was just going to set, and they came upon a small stream. When they were just going to cross the stream, they saw a very beautiful young girl there. One monk who was old, traditional, orthodox, immediately closed his eyes because it is not good to see a woman—desire may arise, just may come in, passion may happen. Just to avoid he closed his eye and moved into the stream.

The other monk who was a young man, newly ordained, not well trained in the orthodoxy of the sect, asked the girl, 'Why are you standing here? The sun is going to set, soon it will be night, and this place is lonely.'

The girl said, 'I am afraid to go into the stream. Can't you help me little? Can't you give me your hand?'

The monk said, 'The stream is deep, it will be better if you come and sit on my shoulder and I will carry you.'

The other monk, the first old monk, reached the other shore, and then he looked back. What was happening? And when he saw that the girl was sitting on the monk's shoulder he became very much disturbed. His mind was revolving fast: 'This is the sin!' He himself also felt guilty, because he was older, senior; he should have told the other young monk to avoid. And this is sin, and he would have to report it to the chief abbot.

The young monk crossed the stream, left the girl there, and started going towards the monastery. The monastery must have been one or two miles away. They walked. The old monk was so angry that he couldn't speak. They walked in silence. Then they reached the door of the monastery, and when they were crossing the door the old monk stopped and said, ' You have done wrong! It is prohibited! You should not have done this!'

The young monk was surprised. He said, 'What ? What are you saying? What have I done? I have remained completely silent. I have not even said a single word.'

—Vedanta: The Supreme Knowledge

The old monk said, ' I am not talking about these two miles you have walked with me. I am talking about that beautiful young girl you were carrying in the stream.'

The young man said, 'But I dropped the girl there, and it seems you are still carrying her.

If a mystic is really a mystic, he cannot carry any division. He cannot say, 'That is outside, and this is inside,' because only ego can divide; ego is the boundary. Only mind n divide, and no-mind cannot divide. Nothing is outside and nothing is in—the whole existence is *advaita*, one, non-dual. Divisibility is not possible—it is oneness, it is harmony, no boundaries exist. But if somebody goes on condemning…

There are monks, millions of monks, all over the world, in Hindu monasteries, in Christian monasteries, in Buddhist monasteries, who are afraid of the outside and who go on condemning it. That shows they are really interested, still interested , them outside—otherwise why condemn? They have a deep unconscious lust for it, otherwise why condemn?

Their condemnation shows they have some deep greed for it. When the greed really disappears; how can there be condemnation? How can you hate the world? The hate is possible if love is somewhere hidden behind. Love and hate are not two things, love-hate is the phenomenon;

120

they are two aspects of the same coin. You can change the aspects: from love you can come to hate. When you were in love with the world, hate was hidden behind; now you hate the world, love is hidden behind—the other aspect remains.

A real mystic is one for whom the coin has disappeared: there is no hate, no love—no hate-love relationship. He simply exists without dividing. And there is no difficulty in it. If you try to make a harmony between the two, then there will be difficulty; if you try somehow to synthesize, then there will be difficulty. You cannot synthesize. This has been tried.

Reading the Upanishad you may come to realize, intellectually of course, that the out and the in are one; within and without are the same. If you realize intellectually, then you will start trying to make a synthesis of the division. In the first place division is wrong; in the second place, to try to synthesize is doubly wrong, because synthesis means that you still think they are divided and somehow they have to be joined. Then it is very difficult, and you synthesis will remain superficial; deep down the division will exist. You can only white-wash it, that's all-you cannot do much.

But it is very simple if you disappear. Then there is no need to synthesize. When you disappear, simply they are one-there is no need to synthesize, there is no need to join them together. They were never apart. They have always been joined, they have always been one. It was you: because of you the division existed.

Many people try many types of synthesis. In India this last century; many people have tried to synthesize all religions, synthesize Christianity, Hinduism, and Mohammedanism, but the whole effort was a failure. It was bound to be a failure, because in the first place he believed in the division—that they are separate—and then he tried a synthesis. The foundation wag that they are separate and they have to be potch thing—not very meaningful, not alive. The real synthesis happens only when you can see there are no divisions. Not that you synthesize—simply you see there are no divisions. There is no need to join them together they have never been apart.

A mystic is one who has disappeared. Through his disappearance, all divisions simply disappear. And I say all divisions, absolutely all divisions. He cannot divide between the good and the bad; he cannot divide between God and the Devil; he cannot divide between hell and heaven—simply he cannot divide. It is not only a question of in and out, because that's very simple. We can think, 'Okay, maybe in and out are the same'—but heaven and hell? Devil and God?

You may not be aware that the English word 'devil' comes from the same root as the word 'divine'. Both come from the Sanskrit root: the Sanskrit root is dev. Dev means god, divine, devata. From dev comes the English word 'divine', and from dev comes the English word 'devil'. Both are divine. Both are one.

Good and bad.... Very difficult to conceive, because the mind persists. How can one think that the bad is also good, and the good is also bad? Look. For a moment try to look into the non-divided reality of things. Can you think of any man who is good if there exists no man who is bad? Can you think of Buddha, Krishna, Christ, without there existing Hitler, Mussolini, Stalin, Napoleon, Alexander? You cannot conceive of it. A Buddha cannot exist without there being someone who is a Genghis Khan, *Tamberlane. *Tamberlane is also impossible, cannot exist, if there exists no Buddha. You just look in your society: the sinner cannot exist without the saint, and the saint cannot exist without the sinner—they are joined together.

Many people come from the West and ask me, 'In India there have been so many saints, but the whole society seems to be of sinners. Why this paradox?' This is not s paradox. This is a simple, obvious fact, this must be so, because saints can exist only amidst sinners. They are not two the more saints, the more sinners. If you want sinners disappear, you will have to destroy saints first: when saints disappear, sinners disappear.

Lao Tzu says in 'Tao-Te-Ching' that when the world was really religious there were no saints. When there were saints immediately sinners appeared. So the saint cannot exist without the sinner. That means they are joined together somehow; they are part of one reality. Make one disappear, and the other will disappear automatically.

It is just like hot and cold. Make hot disappear completely and cold will disappear, because cold is nothing but a degree of hot. Make cold disappear completely and hot will disappear, because the difference is only of degrees, the quality is the same. And saints and sinners are just like hot ,and cold; they are degrees on the same thermometer. Destroy one, the other is destroyed immediately—they exist as polarities. People go on asking, 'If God is good, then why in this world is there evil?' God cannot exist without the evil; the evil is because the God is. The light cannot exist without darkness; neither can the darkness exist without light.

For Christianity, this has been such a big problem that for twenty centuries Christian theologicians have been continuously working on this one problem: why does evil exist if God is good? They have not solved it, and they will never be able to solve it, because they cannot see the simple reality that good and bad are two degrees of the same phenomenon. So they have to divide. They say, 'All good belongs to God, and all bad belongs to the Devil.'

And from where does this Devil come? If the Devil comes from God himself, then why so much fuss about it?—he belongs to God. If the Devil is a separate source, from God, then two Gods exist in this world. And then there is no necessity that the good God will win. The whole situation seems to be otherwise. There is every possibility, if the Devil is also a separate source, that he will win—because ninetynine percent he is winning every day! If they are separate sources then it is better to worship the Devil, because you are on the losing side if you go on worshipping God.

So Christian theologicians cannot say that the Devil is a separate source; they say that the Devil was also an angel of God, but then he disobeyed. They go on shifting the problem. Then from where does this disobedience come? If it comes from the Devil himself, then he becomes a separate source. Or if God himself suggests it to him then it becomes a play, a game.

When I was saying last night that life is a game, a play, and God is playing this whole cosmic joke, one friend immediately wrote a letter, saying that it cannot be conceived that Jesus being crucified is just God's play. The crucifixion of Jesus cannot be conceived as just God's play; it must have some purpose.

The question is not whether any particular thing has some purpose or not; the question is whether the whole has a purpose or not. You are here. You had a purpose in coming here, that I know; without purpose you would not be here. Jesus may have had a purpose, or you may think that he had a purpose. Christians may think that he had a purpose-salvation was the purpose, to liberate humanity from the sin that Adam committed was the purpose. But this is your thinking. If Jesus is enlightened, he cannot have any purpose, because purpose belongs to ignorance. He can only be in a play. And if he also thinks that whatsoever hp is, doing is very serious, purposive, then he belongs to the same business mind as you.

And the whole, the cosmos, cannot have any purpose, use purpose because purpose means something outside. There is nothing outside the whole. And whenever we think that God must have some purpose we are talking in deep absurdities, because if God has any purpose, he is omnipotent so he can do it immediately. Why waste so much time? If he has only this purpose—that man should reach heaven—he can simply order, 'Go to heaven!' Because when he can say, 'Let there be light,' and there is light; when he can say, 'Le there be the world,' and the world is there, then why can' he say, 'Let there be only heaven,' so that everybody is in heaven? Then why this whole nonsense of Adam committing sin, then Jesus helping people? Why this nonsense?

Purpose is absurd in terms of the total. Purpose may exist for individual egos, because egos cannot exist without purpose, but for the cosmic there is no ego. It cannot be anything else than a cosmic play. Even Jesus' crucifixion is a play. That's why Jesus can go to the crucifixion so easily, not disturbed, as if it is just a drama, as if he is just acting a role. The man of knowledge is just an actor enacting a role. What is going to be the result is not his concern. Whatsoever the result, everything is good. There is neither good nor bad, there is neither in nor out, there is neither beginning nor end-but this happens only when you have disappeared.

You can misunderstand me. I am not saying to go and do evil because there is no difference. I am not saying to go and kill somebody because it is just a drama. And if you are really thinking of killing someone, then when you are to jail or killed, murdered by the court, then You will have to enjoy it, it is a game. If you are ready to accept the whole, then you can go and kill. But then don't complain because in a game, in a play, complaining is useless.

To understand this, intellect alone will not be of much help. If can only prepare the ground. Unless your being is transformed, you cannot see this unity; you cannot see this vast unity of polar opposites. They exist together, they disappear together. Gurdjieff used to say an apparently very absurd thing, but deep down a reality. He used to say that everything remains in the same quantity always: the proportion remains the same. The same proportion always remains between saints and sinners. That cannot be disturbed, otherwise the world will lose balance. The same proportion exists between ignorant people and people who are wise— that cannot be disturbed.

Now modern psychology also has discovered a few facts which are relevant. One of them is this: five percent of people, only five percent, are intelligent, talented, genius, and five percent of people are idiotic, stupid—exactly the same proportion. On one polarity five percent with intelligence, on another polarity five percent with complete absence of intelligence. And then there are other grades, and every grade has a proportionate grade on the other side. You can divide the whole world. It is like two polarities balancing each other: whenever something grows more, immediately the balance has to be regained.

It is just like a walker, a tight-rope walker. The tight-rope walker has a trick, a balancing trick. Whenever he feels that he is losing balance and is leaning towards the left and will fall down, immediately he moves to the right. When he feels that he has moved too much to the right and will fall down, he again moves to the left. Walking on the rope, continuously he goes on moving from left to right, from right to left, regaining balance by the opposite.

The same happens in existence: the proportion remains almost the same. Whenever there is born a very saintly person, immediately a sinner is born somewhere. Whenever a wise man is born, immediately one idiot has to balance him, otherwise the world would disappear immediately. Whenever you do a good act, know well that somewhere someone will have to do a bad act to balance you. So don't get too proud that you have done some good acts, because by doing them you have created the other also. Someone has to balance you, because you unbalanced the world. Whenever you do a bad act, someone is bound to become a saint because of you.

I am not saying to do this or that. Upanishads are not concerned with your doing, they are concerned with your understanding—that you understand well that the world exists in duality, and if you go on dividing you will remain a part of ignorance. Don't divide, transcend division, and look at the world as one vast expanse.

Once you know that the two are not two, the opposites are not opposites, you cannot be tense, because tension is possible only when you choose. When you say 'This must be, and that must not be'; when you say 'This is good and 'that is bad', you are creating anguish for yourself. You .will create tension, you will create a conflict within the mind; expectations, hopes, frustrations—all will follow. Once you can understand that no choice is needed because everything is the same, suddenly all anguish disappears. And then you have a tranquillity, a peace, a bliss, that can exist only when divisions have disappeared.

If one experiences or understands inwardly the deep feeling of becoming as a dry leaf to be moved only by the existence itself, then how can one push oneself to breathe or jump or do anything at all but lie flat on the earth and dissolve?

First: to experience and to understand are two different things. If you experience this, there is no need to ask the question—just lie down flat on the ground and dissolve.

Why ask the question? This is an act; you are doing something. No dry leaf has ever asked. But the very question shows that intellectually you understand, but you have not experienced any such thing. And intellectual understanding is not understanding at all. Intellectual understanding is just appearance of understanding; it is not understanding.

Why do I say this? I will read the sentence; you will feel why. If one experiences or understands... You cannot use the 'or', because they are not the same thing—either you experience or you don't experience. First thing: intellectual understanding is not equal to experience.... or understands inwardly the deep feeling of becoming as a dry leaf to be moved only by the existence itself, then how can one push oneself to breathe or jump or do anything at all but lie flat on the earth and dissolve?

You will have to do that also—to lie flat. You will have to do that also—to lie flat on the earth. And if you can do that, why can't you push, jump and breathe?

I will tell you one anecdote. It happened, one Zen monk Doz-en used to tell his disciples, 'Unless you die, you will not be reborn.' So one stupid disciple—and there are always many—thought, 'if this is the key, then I must try.' So one day he came and did just as you have said. He must have lain with closed eyes, flat out in front of the door of the master, just in the morning when the master was expected to come out for the morning prayer.

The master opened the door and found that his disciple was lying there not breathing, as if dead. The master Doz-en said, 'Okay, doing well.' So the disciple opened one eye, just to see the expression on the master's face, and Doz-en said, 'Stupid! Dead men don't open their eyes!'

You will have to do that also—to lie flat on the ground—but that will be your doing. And these breathing exercises are to help you so that it can happen and is not your doing. All these techniques of meditation are to help you to come to this realization when suddenly you feel that it is happening-you have fallen on the ground, dissolving. But that should not be something done on your part; you cannot do it. If it is a doing, the whole point is lost. It must be a spontaneous happening.

And right now, whatsoever you do will not be spontaneous; whatsoever you are doing, you have to make effort. And I know that you have to make effort for breathing, for catharsis, for the mantra hoo—and you have to bring all effort possible. These efforts are not going to become your enlightenment, because enlightenment is never achieved through effort, but these efforts will help you: they will bring you to a point where you can become effortless. And when you become effortless, enlightenment is always there. You can stop them, but just by stopping them nothing will happen. Continue them, and do them as totally as possible, because then you will come to realize sooner that nothing can be achieved through effort.

Nothing can be achieved through effort—you have to realize this. I can say this, but this will not be of much help. I know well that just by breathing fast, you are not going to enter into nirvana. I know it well. And just by crying and dancing, no one has ever entered there. Even if their door is open, they will close it. If they see that you are coming doing dynamic meditation, they will close the door. This I know well.

I have heard. One Christian missionary was giving a sermon to some middle-school students, small boys and girls. After the sermon he asked, 'Those who want to go to heaven should raise their hands.' So all the boys, except one, raised their hands. Only one boy, someone called Johnny, remained silent.

The missionary asked, 'Don't you want to go to heaven?' Johnny said, 'Not with this bunch!'

So if you go doing dynamic meditation, even I cannot enter with you, it is impossible. But I know that dynamic meditation is not the end. It is just to prepare you so that you can drop automatically. It is to exhaust you and your ego; it is to exhaust your mind, your body; it is to exhaust your individuality. And when your individuality is exhausted completely, you will drop on the ground like a dry leaf. But not like Doz-en's disciple. If he could have done dynamic meditation, the whole story would have been different. Then there would have been no need to lie down on the ground; he would have fallen on the ground.

And if you have to lie down, that shows only that you are withholding yourself, you are not really exhausted. If you simply move totally in whatsoever I am saying to do, you will get exhausted. You have a certain amount of energy, a, limited amount of energy—that energy can be exhausted. Once exhausted you will become a dry leaf, a dead leaf.

When you cannot do anything, only then can non-doing happen While you can do something, non-doing is not possible.

Does returning to the heart center mean becoming more passionate? Is the heart also the source of passion? Can a man who is authentically centered at the heart be called passionate?

Heart is not the center of passion, rather, heart is the center of compassion. And the man who lives in the heart cannot be called passionate, but can be called compassionate. Passion comes from the sex center; all passion comes from the sex center. You can join the sex center and the heart, but from the heart only love flows, not passion.

Love is a very silent flow, non-aggressive, almost-passive. It is a very silent breeze. Sex is passion, violence, aggression, with force, with strong energy—it attacks. The heart and the sex center can join together, then love becomes passionate. If heart is not joined with the sex center, then love becomes compassionate. Then love is there in its total purity, and only then, when there is no passion in it, is love pure. It is silent, passive, non-aggressive. You can invite it, but it will not knock at your door. It will not even ask to be invited. You can persuade it to come, it can become your guest, but it will not come uninvited.

Love cannot rape, and sex always rapes in many ways. Even when legally it is not a rape, sex is rape. You may persuade the other person legally, in the way the society allows, but in the mind tape remains the center. You are just thinking to rape the other person, you are aggressive, and all that you do before it is just a foreplay, just to achieve the end. That's why, when two, persons get married, foreplay disappears.

When you meet a girl or a boy for the first time, there is much foreplay! Before you enter into a sex relationship you have to go on playing, so that the sex doesn't look like a rape, but that is on the mind, that is in the mind. In your mind you are constantly thinking of the end, and everything is just persuasion, seduction, just to make the whole thing appear loving. But the more you become intimate with the girl or the boy, less and less is there foreplay; if you get married, no foreplay. Then sex becomes just direct; something to be done and finished with.

Look at this. If two persons are really in love, then not only foreplay but afterplay also will be there. If two persons are not in love then sex will happen and they will go to sleep, there will be no afterplay. Foreplay will not even by there, and afterplay is impossible, because what is the use? The thing has happened, the end has been achieved. Rape is in the mind.

The sex center knows only rape; it is the center of aggression. That's why the military don't allow sex for soldiers, because if they have sex relationships they cannot be good fighters. The aggression moves through the sex center. If sex is allowed and a soldier is living with his wife or with his beloved, he will not feel like, fighting on the battleground.

This is one of the reasons why American soldiers are defeated everywhere: their girls follow them. They cannot be aggressive, because the center of aggression is sex. If sex is allowed, aggression flows out of you, and then you don't like fighting. So the soldiers have to be prohibited sex, they must suppress their sex. Then the whole sex becomes aggression. Then, rather than entering a woman's body, they can enter anybody's body with a bullet. But it is the same thing——the entry. Your bullets, your knives, your guns, are just phallic symbols—to enter the other's body, to destroy.

The coaches of athletes who go to the Olympics tell them, 'Don't have sex at least for two weeks,' because if you have sex you will not be a good runner. From where will you get the aggression to fight and run and complete? All religions all over the world-almost all, I will say, because only one wonderful sect, *Tantra*, is an exception—all religions all over the world have told their monks to be celibate, because they think that religion is also a sort of struggle. You have to fight with yourself, so retain the aggressive energy and fight with yourself.

Sex can easily become violence because it is passion, it is rape. Love, the heart center or the love center, is totally different. It is non-violent, it is passive, not even active. It can come to you like a very silent perfume, and that too when you invite. That's why persons like Buddha or Jesus, they have much love, but we cannot feel their love, because we can feel love only when it is too violent. We have become addicted to vilence. And Buddha's love is so silen. It showers on us but we cannot feel it, We have become so insensitive. Only when someone attacks do we start feeling.

The heart center is not the center of passion, but is the center of compassion. And compassion is absolutely different from passion, just the opposite. It is non-aggressive energy, moving without any noise, but you have to become very sensitive to feel it. So only very sensitive persons can become attracted to Buddha, because only very sensitive persons can feel that some love is flowing from him. If you are asking for strong doses of passion, then Buddha will just look dead, nothing is coming out of him.

Remember this: passion has to be transformed into compassion, only then will you move from the sex center to the heart center. Now even your heart has to follow your sex center, which is the higher following the lower. Then your sex center will follow the love center, the heart center—the lower following the higher. Then the lower becomes totally different, the quality changes.

When sex follows love, sex becomes beautiful, a grace, a blessing. When love follows sex, love becomes ugly, a destructive force; you destroy each other through your love. All the courts of the world are filled with persons who have been in love and now are destructive to each other. Fifty fifty percent of marriages brack down completlely, and the other fifty percent are continued somehow, not for love, but for other reasons—for children, for society, for family, for prestige, for money for other reasons, but not for love. Fifty percent break down completely.

Love has become so destructive because it is following a lower center. Remember, this should be the law within you: always remember that the lower should follow the higher then everything is beautiful and a blessing. Nothing is to be denied, there is no need to deny anything, only let the higher lead because following the higher, the lower changes its quality. And if the higher has to follow the lower, everything becomes ugly.

Did Mulla Nasrudin become enlightened?

He must have—because if he is not enlightened, then nobody can be.

Mulla Nasrudin is a Sufi figure, one of the oldest centers of Sufi anecdotes, and he shows whatsoever I have been saying here: that the world is a cosmic joke—he represents that. He is a very serious joker, and if you can penetrate him and understand him, then many mysteries will be revealed to you.

Mulla Nasrudin illustrates that the world is not a tragedy, but a comedy. And the world is a place where if you can learn how to laugh, you have learned everything. If your prayer cannot become a deep laughter which comes from all over your being, if your prayer is sad and if you cannot joke with your god, then you are not really religious.

Christians, Jews and Mohammedans are very serious about their god; Hindus are not, they have joked a lot. And that shows how much they believe, because when you cannot joke with your god you don't believe in him. You feel that through your humour, your joke, he will be insulted. Your belief is shallow; it is not deep enough. Hindus say that the trust is so much that they can laugh; the trust is so much that just by laughing it cannot be broken.

One Buddhist, Bodhidharma, one of the greatest followers of Buddha, used to say to his disciples, 'Whenever you take the name of Buddha, immediately rinse out your mouth, because this name is dangerous and it makes the mouth impure.' Another Buddhist monk, Bokuju, used to tell his disciples, 'While meditating, if this fellow Gautam Buddha comes in, kill him immediately, because once you allow him then he will cling to you and it will be difficult to be alone.' And they were great followers, they loved Buddha—but they could laugh. Why? The love was so intimate; so close, that there was no danger that something might be taken wrongly. But Christians have always been afraid, so immediately anything becomes blasphemy—anything. They cannot take anything humorously, and if you cannot take anything humorously, if you cannot laugh at yourself, at your god, then you are ill, you are not at home, and your god is something to be feared.

In English we have a word, 'god-fearing', for religious people. A god-fearing person can never be religious, because if you fear God you cannot love him. Love and fear cannot exist together. With fear, hate can exist, love cannot with fear, anger can exist, love cannot; with fear you can bow down, but you cannot surrender; with fear you can be a relationship between a slave and a master, but there cannot be a love relationship. Hindus, Buddhists have a totally different attitude, and that attitude is different because they think the whole existence is a cosmic play; you can be playful.

Sufis are very playful; they created Mulla Nasrudin. And Mulla Nasrudin is an alive figure, you can go on adding to Mulla Nasrudin is an alive figure, you can go on adding to him. . . I go on adding. If someday he meets me there is bound to be difficulty, because I go on creating around him. To me he is a constantly alive figure, in many ways symbolic— symbolic of human stupidity. But he knows it andhe laugh at it and whenever he behaves like a stupid man, he is just joking at you, at human beings at large.

And he is subtle enough. He will not hit you directly. He hits himself; but if you can penetrate him, then you can look at the reality. And sometimes even great scriptures cannot go as deep as a joke can go, because the joke directly touches the heart. A scripture goes into the head, into the intellect; a joke directly touches the heart. Immediately something explodes within you and becomes your smile and your laughter.

Nasrudin must have attained enlightenment, or he is already an enlightened figure, there is no need to attain. I go on using him just to give you a feeling that to me religious is not serious. So I go on mixing Mulla Nasrudin with Mahavir—which is impossible, poles apart. I go on mixing Mulla Nasrudin with the Upanishads, because he give a sweetness to the whole serious thing. And nothing is serious, nothing should be serious.

To me, to laugh wholeheartedly is the greatest celebration that can happen to a man—to laugh wholeheartedly, to become the laughter. Then no meditation is needed, it is enough.

I will take one or two anecdotes from Nasrudin.

Once it happened that Nasrudin and his friend, Sheik Abdullah, lost their way in a forest. They tried and tried to find their way, but then evening came, the night was descending, so they had to wait for the whole night under a tree it was dangerous ground, there were many wild animals, and they had to keep awake, because any moment they could be killed.

They tried every way to keep awake, but Mulla was tired, yawning, feeling sleepy, so he said to Skeikh Abdullah, 'Invent something, because

I am feeling sleepy and it seems impossible now to stay awake. The whole day we were traveling, and I am tired.'

Sheikh Abdullah asked, 'What should I do?' Nasrudin said, 'We should play a game, a game of guessing. You describe a film actress-just become the film actress and describe—and I will guess who this film actress is. Then I will do the same and you guess.

Even Abdullah became interested, it seemed to be a good game. So Abdullah said, 'Okay'. He contemplated and then he said, 'My eyes are like Noor Jahan, my nose is like Cleopatra, my lips like Marilyn Monroe', and so on and so forth.

Mulla Nasrudin became very excited, his blood pressure rose high. Even in the dark you could have seen his eyes, they became so fiery. And then when Sheikh Abdullah said, 'Now, the measurements of my body— 36-24-36'. Nasrudin jumped over to Sheikh Abdullah. Sheikh Abdullah said, 'Wait, guess!'

Nasrudin said, 'Who is bothered about guessing? I don't care who you are. Quick! Kiss me!'

The human mind is such—imagination, desire, passion, projection. You project, you imagine, and then you become the victim. And this is not a joke, this is reality—and this is about you.

●●●

Osho International Meditation Resort

Every year the Osho International Meditation Resort welcomes thousands of people from over 100 countries who come to enjoy a holiday in an atmosphere of meditation and celebration. The 40-acre resort is located about 100 miles southeast of Mumbai (Bombay), in Pune, India, in a tree-lined residential area set against a backdrop of bamboo groves and wild jasmine, peacocks and waterfalls.

The basic approach of the resort is that of Zorba the Buddha: living in awareness, with a capacity to celebrate everything in life. Many visitors come to just be, to allow themselves the luxury of doing nothing. Others choose to participate in a wide variety of courses and sessions that support moving toward a more joyous and less stressful life by combining methods of self-understanding with awareness techniques. These courses are offered through Osho Multiversity and take place in a pyramid complex next to the famous Osho Teerth zen gardens.

You can choose to practice various meditation methods, both active and passive, from a daily schedule that begins at six o'clock in the morning. Each evening there is a meditation event that moves from dance to silent sitting, using Osho's recorded talks as an opportunity to experience inner silence without effort.

Facilities include tennis courts, a gym, sauna, Jacuzzi, a nature-shaped Olympic-sized swimming pool, classes in zen archery, tai chi, chi gong, yoga and a multitude of bodywork session. The kitchen serves international gourmet vegetarian meals, made with organically grown produce. The nightlife is alive with friends dining under the stars, with music and dancing.

Make online bookings for accommodation at the new Osho Guesthouse inside the resort through the website below or drop us an email at guesthouse@osho.com.

Take an online tour of the meditation resort, and access travel and program information at: www.osho.com/resort

BOOKS BY OSHO

EARLY DISCOURSES AND WRITINGS
A Cup of Tea
Dimensions Beyond The Known
From Sex to Superconsciousness
The Great Challenge
Hidden Mysteries
I Am The Gate
Psychology of the Esoteric
Seeds of Wisdom

MEDITATION
And Now and Here (Vol. 1 & 2)
in Search of the Miraculous (Vol. 1 & 2)
Meditation: The Art of Ecstasy
Meditation: The First and Last Freedom
Vigyan Bhairav Tantra
(boxed 2-volume set with 112 meditation cards)
Yaa-Hoo! The Mystic Rose

BUDDHA AND BUDDHIST MASTERS
The Dhammapada (Vol. 1 - 2)
The Way of the Buddha
The Diamond Sutra
The Discipline of Transcendence (Vol. 1-4)
The Heart Sutra The Book of Wisdom
(combined edition of Vol. 1 & 2)

BAUL MYSTICS
The Beloved (Vol. 1 & 2)

KABIR
The Divine Melody
Ecstasy: The Forgotten Language
The Fish in the Sea in Not Thirsty
The Great Secret
The Guest
The Path of Love
The Revolution

JESUS AND CHRISTIAN MYSTICS
Come Follow to You (Vol. 1-4)
I Say Unto You (Vol. 1 & 2)
The Mustard Seed
Theologia Mystica

JEWISH MYSTICS
The Art of Dying
The True Sage

WESTERN MYSTICS
Guida Spirituale *On the Desiderata*
The Hidden Harmony
The Fragments of Heraclitus
The Messiah (Vol. 1 & 2) *Commentaries on*

The Grass Grows By Itself
The Great Zen Master Ta Hui
Hsin Hsin Ming: The Book of Nothing
Discourses on the Faith-Mind of Sosan
I Celebrate Myself: God is No Where, Life is Now Here
Kyozan: A True Man of Zen
Nirvana: The Last Nightmare
No Mind : The Flowers of Eternity
No Water, No Moon
One Seed Makes the Whole Earth Green
Returning to the Source
The Search: Talks on the 10 Bulls of Zen
A Sudden Clash of Thunder
The Sun Rises in the Evening
Take it Easy (Vol 1) *Poems of Ikkyu*
Take it Easy (Vol 2) *Poems of Ikkyu*
This Very Body the Buddha *Hakuin's Song of Meditation*
Walking in Zen, Sitting in Zen
The White Lotus
Yakusan: Straight to the Point of Enlightment
Zen Manifesto: Freedom From Oneself
Zen: The Mystery and the Poetry of the Beyond
Zen: The Path of Paradox (Vol. 1, 2 & 3)
Zen: The Special Transmission

ZEN BOXED SETS
The World of Zen (5 volumes)
Live Zen
This. This. A Thousand Times This
Zen: The Diamond Thunderbolt
Zen: The Quantum Leap from Mind to No-Mind
Zen: The Solitary Bird Cuckoo of the Forest
Zen: All the Colors of the Rainbow (5 Vol.)
The Buddha : The Emptiness of the Heart
The Language of Existence
The Miracle
The Original Man
Turning in
Osho: On the Ancient Masters of Zen (7 Vol.)
Dogen: The Zen Master
Hyakujo: The Everest of Zen- With Basho's haikus
Isan: No Footprints in the Blue Sky
Joshu: The Lion's Roar
Ma Tzu: The Empty Mirror
Nansen: The Point of Departure
Rinzai: Master of the Irrational
* Each volume is also available individually.

RESPONES TO QUESTIONS
Be Still and Know
Come, Come, Yet Again Come
The Goose is Out
The Great Pilgrimage: From Here to Here
The Invitation
My Way: The Way of the White Clouds
Nowhere to Go But In
The Razor's Edge
Walk Without Feet, Fly Without Wings and Think Without Mind
The Wild Geese and the Water
Zen : Zest, Zip, Zap and Zing

Khalil Gibran's *The Prophet*
The New Alchemy: To Turn You On
Commentaries on Mabel Collins'
Light on the Path
Philosophia Perennis (Vol. 1 & 2)
The Golden Verses of Pythagoras
Zarathustra: A God That Can Dance
Zarathustra: The Laughing Prophet
Commentaries on Nietzsche's
Thus Spake Zarathustra

SUFISM
Just like That
Journey to the Heart (same as Until You Die)
The Perfect Master (Vol. 1 & 2)
The Secret
Sufis: The People of the Path (Vol. 1 & 2)
Unio Mystica (Vol. 1 & 2)
The Wisdom of the Sands (Vol. 1 & 2)

TANTRA
Tantra: The Supreme Understanding
The Tantra Experience
The Royal Song of Saraha
(*same as* Tantra Vision, Vol.1)
The Tantric Transformation
The Royal Song of Saraha
(*same as* Tantra Vision, Vol.2)

THE UPANISHADS
Heartbeat of the Absolute
Ishavasya Upanishad
I Am That *Isa Upanishad*
Philosophia Ultima *Mandukya Upanishad*
The Supreme Doctrine *Kenopanishad*

Finger Pointing to the Moon
Adhyatma Upanishad
That Art Thou *Sarvasar Upanishad,*
Kaivalya Upanishad, Adhyatma
Upanishad
The Ultimate Alchemy
Atma Pooja Upanishad (Vol. 1 & 2)
Vedanta: Seven Steps to Samadhi
Akshaya Upanishad

TAO
The Empty Boat
The Secret of Secrets
Tao: The Golden Gate
Tao: The Pathless Path
Tao: The Three Treasures
When the Shoes Fits

YOGA
Yoga: The Alpha and the Omega (Vol. 1-
10)

ZEN AND ZEN MASTERS
Ah, This!
Ancient Music in the Pines
And the Flowers Showered
A Bird on the Wing
(same as Roots and Wings)
Bodhidharma: The Greatest Zen Master
Communism and Zen Fire, Zen Wind
Dang Dang Doko Dang
The First Principle
God is Dead: Now Zen is the only Living
Truth

The Sound of One Hand Clapping
The Sun Behind the Sun Behind the Sun
The Tongue - Tip Taste of Tao
This Is It
Turn On, Tune In and Drop the Lot
What Is, Is, What Ain't Ain't
Won't You Join The Dance?

COMPILATIONS
Bhagwan Shree Rajneesh: On Basic Human Rights
Jesus Crucified Again, This Time in Ronald Reagans America
Priests and Politicians: The Mafia of the Soul

GIFT BOOKS OF OSHO QUOTATIONS
A Must for Contemplation Before Sleep
A Must for Morning Contemplation
Gold Nuggets
More Gold Nuggets
Words From a Man of No Words
At the Feet of the Master

PHOTOBOOKS
Shree Rajneesh : A Man of Many Climates, Seasons and Rainbows *through the eye of the camera*

Impressions.... *Osho Commune Internation Photobook*

BOOKS ABOUT OSHO
Bhagwan: The Buddha for the Future
by Juliet Forman, S.R.N., S.C.M., R.M.N.
Bhagwan ·Shree Rajneesh: The Most Dangerous Man Since Jesus Christ
by Sue Appleton, LL.B., M.A.B.A.
Bhagwan: The Most Godless Yet the Most Godly Man *by Dr. George Meredith, M.D. M.B.B.S. M.R.C.P.*
Bhagwan: One Man Against the Whole Ugly Past of Humanity *by Juliest Forman, S.R.N., S.C.M., R.M.N.*
Bhagwan: Twelve Days That Shook the World *by Juliet Forman, S.R.N., S.C.M., R.M.N.*
Was Bhagwan Shree Rajneesh Poisoned by Ronald Reagan's America?
by Sue Appleton, LL.B. M.A.B.A.
Diamond Days With Osho
by Ma Prem Shunyo

GIFTS
Zorba the Buddha Cookbook

For Osho Books & Audio/Video Tapes Contact:
SADHANA FOUNDATION
17, KOREGAON PARK, PUNE-411001, MS, INDIA
PH: 020-66019999, FAX: 020-66019990
E-mail: resortinfo@osho.net
Internet Website: http://www.osho.com